W9-BPQ-590

Shaunti and Jeff Feldhahn

For Women Only

For Men Only and

For Couples Only

Participant's Guide

3-in-1 Relationship Study Resource

MULTNOMAH
BOOKS

FOR WOMEN ONLY, FOR MEN ONLY, AND FOR COUPLES ONLY PARTICIPANT'S GUIDE
PUBLISHED BY MULTNOMAH BOOKS
12265 Oracle Boulevard, Suite 200
Colorado Springs, Colorado 80921

All Scripture quotations are taken from the Holy Bible, New Living Translation, copyright © 1996, 2004, 2007. Used by permission of Tyndale House Publishers Inc., Carol Stream, Illinois 60188. All rights reserved.

Details in some anecdotes and stories have been changed to protect the identities of the persons involved.

Portions of *Guide 1* and *Guide 2* in this book appeared in different versions in the standalone books *For Women Only Discussion Guide* by Shaunti Feldhahn with Lisa A. Rice, copyright © 2006 by Veritas Enterprises Inc., and *For Men Only Discussion Guide* by Shaunti and Jeff Feldhahn with Brian Smith, copyright © 2007 by Veritas Enterprises Inc., both published by Multnomah Books.

Trade Paperback ISBN 978-1-60142-474-7
eBook ISBN 978-1-60142-480-8

Cover design by Mark D. Ford

Published in association with the literary agency of Calvin Edwards, 1220 Austin Glen Drive, Atlanta, GA 30338.

Published in the United States by WaterBrook Multnomah, an imprint of the Crown Publishing Group, a division of Random House Inc., New York.

MULTNOMAH and its mountain colophon are registered trademarks of Random House Inc.

Printed in the United States of America
2013—First Edition

10 9 8 7 6 5 4 3 2 1

SPECIAL SALES
Most WaterBrook Multnomah books are available at special quantity discounts when purchased in bulk by corporations, organizations, and special-interest groups. Custom imprinting or excerpting can also be done to fit special needs. For information, please e-mail SpecialMarkets@ WaterBrookMultnomah.com or call 1-800-603-7051.

Contents

About the 3-in-1 Relationship Study Resource

Have you ever looked at the person you know and love best in the world, heard something shocking about how that person thinks, and wondered, *Wait—how have I not heard this before?*

A decade ago, we stumbled upon some key things that we didn't know about each other. After investigating them, publishing them in our books *For Women Only* and *For Men Only,* and seeing how life changing they are, we think it is important for everyone else to know them too. As men and women, we each have certain specific things that we need and a few hidden things that hurt us. But because men and women are wired so differently, we often have no idea what those things are for the person we love. Because the other person is just different, we are often trying hard in the wrong areas. So the other person may not feel cared for the way we expect—or, worse, we can sometimes hurt the other person without ever meaning to.

But once our eyes are opened to what matters to the opposite sex, we can try hard in the *right* areas. We can show we care, we can avoid these unrecognized hurts, and suddenly we may see the other person *feeling* very cared for in the way we wanted all along.

Which Study Should You Do?

This book contains three different guides packaged together.

- Guide 1: The *For Women Only Discussion Guide* is designed to be used by women who are using the *For Women Only* book, the video study, or both the book and the video. Women's groups, Bible studies, and book clubs—any just-us-girls environment—will learn to understand men— husbands, boyfriends, coworkers, sons, or any other men in their lives.

- Guide 2: The *For Men Only Discussion Guide* is designed to be used by men who are using the *For Men Only* book, the video study, or both. Similarly, men will find this guide helpful regardless of whether they are married, dating, or just wanting to understand the alien gender.

- Guide 3: The *For Couples Only Discussion Guide* is a little different. Unlike the other two studies, this one is designed to be done by married, engaged, or dating couples. The key is that in this study men and women will be together the whole time. This study brings together much of the content from the other two studies—not only to unveil what you need to know about your other half, but to help him or her realize what you don't already know (which can be just as important). And it is designed to give the two of you a common language to talk about some key things going forward. Like the others, this particular guide can be used with the books (both *For Women Only* and *For Men Only*), the *For Couples Only* video study, or both.

Whichever study (or studies) you choose to complete, we hope you will have many "Aha!" moments along the way—simple surprises that have big impacts—together with more delight in your relationship and (if you are married) more harmony in your home.

Enjoy the journey!

Jeff and Shaunti Feldhahn

P.S. Please note that these guides are designed to accompany the revised and updated (2013) book versions of *For Men Only* and *For Women Only*. (If you have the older versions of the books, be aware that the page numbers will be different and they each have one less chapter.)

Guide 1

For Women Only

Discussion Guide

Shaunti Feldhahn with Lisa A. Rice

Guide 1 Contents

How to Use the *For Women Only* Discussion Guide

Since the original version of *For Women Only* came out nearly a decade ago, I have been so grateful to hear from women all over the country who tell me, "My eyes have been opened—and I can't believe I didn't know some of these things before!" That excitement is inevitably followed by, "So, um, how do I apply this to *my* life?" This discussion guide will help you do just that; it has been revised and updated to match the 2013 updated edition of *For Women Only*. (Note: Throughout this guide I often use the abbreviation *FWO* for *For Women Only*.)

How to Use This Guide

This guide is designed to be flexible so it can be used in a women's discussion group or as a helpful road map for a good one-on-one dialogue with the man in your life. It can be used with either the *For Women Only* video study, the *FWO* book alone, or both together. The discussion elements (questions, "Life Story" case studies, and so on) are designed to be mixed and matched; pick and choose what works best for your group and your time frame. You can find some helpful suggestions from two different types of groups on the "Studies" portion of our website, www.shaunti.com.

We have found that female audiences, whether married, dating, or single, often experience invaluable "Aha!" moments as they go through this study. I'm primarily focusing on helping apply these truths to romantic relationships, but many of these "Aha!" moments can be useful in other relationships, such as with a son or a male colleague. You'll find that I use the words *guy, man,* and *husband* somewhat interchangeably. (The only exception is that I use *husband* when discussing sex, since I agree with the biblical principle of reserving physical intimacy for marriage.)

You'll notice at the end of each group discussion a section titled "Bringing It Home." The section has questions you and your man can discuss together privately.

Are You Using Just the Book? Video Study? Both?

You can use this guide with either the book or the video study. Or, even better, you can use both together. Here are a few guidelines.

If You Are Using Just the Book

This is probably the simplest way to use this guide, since it is laid out in the same order as the book itself. Thus, chapter 2 in this guide corresponds to chapter 2 in the book.

If You Are Going Through the Video Study

The *For Women Only* video study is organized in six, roughly fifteen-minute video sessions that cover all the topics of the book. Each video includes two to three minutes of interviews with guys explaining how they think. If you are pressed for time, simply skip those interviews.

Fitting the topics into six sessions required a bit of combining and reordering, so you will follow this order:

Video	FWO Book and Guide
Session 1: Insecurity	Chapter 3
Session 2: Respect	Chapter 2
Session 3: Processing / Providing	Chapter 4 / Chapter 5
Session 4: Sex	Chapter 6
Session 5: Visual (includes brief note about Appearance)	Chapter 7 (and Chapter 9)
Session 6: Romance / Words for Your Heart	Chapter 8 / Chapter 10

If You Are Using Both the Book and the Videos

You can use the book as the primary resource, with the video as a supplement, or vice versa; you'll just need to decide which order you will follow.

A note to group leaders: At the beginning of each of the studies in this guide, we indicate which video session and book chapter are covered in that lesson. As noted, several of the video sessions cover multiple topics. So if you are doing this study in the order of the book chapters, not the video sessions, pay attention to what part of the video you are directed to watch so you don't give away the surprise by playing a part of a video that corresponds to a different subject.

The For Women Only Covenant

No matter what process you use, at the end of the study, take a few minutes to think through and fill out the Final Challenge on page 49 for what you will do going forward. As part of that step, don't forget to affirm the For Women Only Covenant together as a group (or on your own as an individual), and post it where it will serve as a reminder in the weeks to come.

A Note About the Emotional Process, Not Just the Physical One

As you read and discuss all these truths about men, please remember that *For Women Only* is not an equal treatment of male-female differences, nor does this guide delve into what guys need to understand about us or what they should do differently. For right now, this is solely about helping us understand the inner lives of men and how we relate to them. Ultimately, it is not supposed to help us change our guy—these revelations are supposed to change and improve us! And in doing so, we will often see the remarkable emergence of the relationship we most wanted all along.

Many have found that the data in *For Women Only* sometimes goes against decades of assumptions about men, and you will likely feel the gamut of emotions as various facts and truths hit you. Please be careful about unloading these emotions on your man. When you do discuss these things with him, remember that it is all too easy for a man to feel insecure and attacked. He will respond much better if he feels that you are respecting him—which, as we will soon learn, is his highest need anyway.

Your Love Is Not Enough

Why Your Respect Means More to Him than Even Your Affection

Your respect means more to your man than even your affection. Three out of four men would rather feel alone and unloved than inadequate and disrespected. Men need to be respected—in public and in private—in their judgment, abilities, communication, and assumptions. It's not about male pride; it's about assuaging feelings of inadequacy. And your man's highest need is feeling that you believe in him, regardless. You can help by assuming the best and choosing to demonstrate respect even in the face of mistakes, just as you want him to love you unconditionally.

For this discussion: Read chapter 2 in the *FWO* book, and/or watch session 2 of the *FWO* video study.

Key Questions

1. How do you talk about your man to your family? to your friends? to his friends?

2. Relate an example of a time you conveyed disrespect to a man—even if you didn't mean to. Also, give an example of when you got it right.

3. What words or actions could most show your man how much you trust, admire, and respect him?

From the Video Study

One man says, "There is a misconception that a man's greatest need is sex.... That's baloney. A man's greatest need is respect.... If that person he desires respect from the most does not respect him, it tears at the core of who he is."

Q Have you ever held the misconception that this man refers to? Have you changed your mind about that, and if so, why?

Q Consider the men you know well. What have you seen (if anything) that signals to you that this man's statement (about respect being vital and disrespect being painful) applies to them as well?

Life Story

Nicole and Blake were on a beach vacation with their family and signed up for a shark-watching tour. However, Blake didn't feel their youngest child—three-year-old Josh—was mature enough to come along. Nicole was angry. She didn't want to deprive any of her children of such a memorable adventure, and she didn't want to leave Josh behind to spend a boring day with a baby-sitter. The couple had a major argument, with Nicole telling Blake, "I can respect you when you're doing well and drawing the children into life, but not when you're making your decisions out of fear."

Blake answered, "So you've chosen to trust me, what, about half the time?"

Life Story Questions

1. What did Nicole do wrong, if anything? What would have been the ideal response from Nicole?

2. Put yourself in Blake's shoes for a moment. What would you feel as the recipient of Nicole's "I can respect you when…" comment? What might be some of the reasons he didn't want Josh to come?

3. How were the words *respect* and *trust* interchangeable in the above scenario? Do you think these terms are synonymous to your man?

Bringing It Home
Discussing It with Your Man

- What in my actions or words most makes you feel respected and appreciated? disrespected and unappreciated?
- To help me see this, can you give me an example of a time I really made you feel trusted? a time when you felt that I didn't trust you?
- Confidentially, which of the couples we know have respectful behavior patterns and which do not?

The **Big** Idea

The one main idea I'm taking away from this week's discussion is:

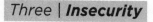

The Performance of a Lifetime

Why Your Mr. Smooth Looks So Impressive but Feels like an Impostor

Despite their in-control exteriors, men often feel like impostors and are insecure because they fear their inadequacies will be discovered. Men believe they're being watched and judged constantly, and three out of four men surveyed admit to feigning confidence despite feelings of inadequacy. Yet the conquering part of men loves the challenge. The key for women is constant affirmation and the creation of a safety zone at home.

For this discussion: Read chapter 3 in the *FWO* book, and/or watch session 1 of the *FWO* video study.

Key Questions

1. What surprised you most about this chapter? Thinking back, how have you seen this self-doubt or insecurity in a man you know?

2. Describe a time when you unintentionally made a man feel *more* insecure, not less. Explain an opportunity you had to affirm him and counteract his secret self-doubt.

3. What can you do to create an affirming safe haven for the guy you love?

From the Video Study

Many men said something like, "I want to tackle a challenge; I want to do great things.... I want to be a good husband (good father, good worker, or whatever), but I'm really not sure I know exactly what I'm doing as a husband (or a father or a worker)—and I hope nobody finds out!"

Q   How do you feel as you learn that guys who live with this imposter complex are often then looking to a wife or girlfriend (or, if they are young, a mom) for the answer to "Do I measure up?"

Q   Is this a question to which they should be seeking the answer only from God? Or do we have a part to play?

Q   How can we best affirm our guys in these often-secret, rarely expressed areas of vulnerability?

Life Story

Last summer Nicole and Blake were out with their new friends Sam and Gayle. At one point Blake suggested that the foursome go boating at a nearby lake. Knowing that her husband disliked boating and the motion sickness he usually felt, Gayle piped up, "Oh, we'd better not. Sam's not a strong swimmer, and he avoids boats like the plague." The others quickly made some alternative suggestions, but they could see that Sam was angry with his wife. Gayle loved her husband dearly and made frequent attempts to turn potentially embarrassing situations light and funny, but something obviously wasn't working.

Life Story Questions

1. What did Gayle do wrong, if anything, regarding Sam?

2. Put yourself in Sam's shoes. How does he view Gayle's attempts to be helpful?

3. What could she have done differently?

Bringing It Home
Discussing It with Your Man

- Read the story on pages 49–50 of *For Women Only*. Have you ever felt like Jean-Luc Picard? Do you ever feel that way at home? elsewhere?
- Can you give me an example of a time I made you feel inadequate? a time I made you feel like you could do it?
- Do you consider our home a haven of unconditional acceptance? Is there anything I could change to make it more so?
- As I learn, will you help me get this by pointing out when I do or say something that makes you feel bad about yourself?

The **Big** Idea

The one main idea I'm taking away from this week's discussion is:

The Thinker

When Checking Out Is Actually Checking In

In a conflict, women tend to want to talk things out immediately, whereas men often want to retreat. Women may view the retreat as a lack of love, but, ironically, the opposite is usually true: men want to engage but need to pull away and have time to process in order to talk about it later. Due to their brain wiring, it is often difficult for men (unlike women) to think things through while talking them through. Especially when emotions are running high, men may feel like deer in the headlights or like they can't properly make their case if they have not had enough processing time. Giving them that time is usually difficult for us, but if we do, we usually will end up with much better communication—and a much better outcome.

For this discussion: Read chapter 4 in the *For Women Only* book, and/or watch the first half of session 3 of the *For Women Only* video study.

Key Questions

1. Give an example of when you unintentionally pressured your guy for an immediate response to an emotional issue. Give an example

of when you allowed him time and space to process. Talk about the difference in outcomes.

2. Consider: What would it feel like to be in a close relationship with someone you cared about deeply if you felt you couldn't keep up verbally when emotions were running high? How does it make you feel knowing this is likely the reality for the men you know?

3. What can you do to create a safe environment for your man to process his thoughts and feelings—including during times of conflict—but still come to the resolution *you* need at some point?

From the Video Study

I explain, "Guys do think about *everything*. They just do it differently than we do." And the men in the video said, "Sometimes it takes a man a while to soak things in," "I need to think and analyze before I can give you an answer," and "I want to say, 'Don't pressure me. I really am thinking about it. I just need time.'"

Q How have you seen your guy go underground to think and do this sort of internal chess match before he gives an answer? What does that look like on the outside? Are there any observable clues when he needs that processing space?

Q If you have done this, how have you pressured him without
realizing the truth about his wiring in this area, and what can
you do to change your responses to him?

Life Story

Blake put down his pen and calculator and leaned back in his chair,
sighing. He dreaded the inevitable conversation he would have with
Nicole.

Sure enough, Nicole soon stormed into the house, taking a
deep breath as she paced the floor. "So I found out today that you
took ten thousand dollars of our savings and opened up an IRA,"
Nicole said. Blake nodded. Nicole continued, "I earmarked most of
that money for a household project—almost a year ago—and you
agreed, I thought. What are you thinking, and why didn't you talk
to me?"

Blake got up and grabbed his jacket and car keys. "I have an
errand to run," he said, "so let's make a date to talk about this
later."

"When, exactly?" Nicole almost shrieked as she followed Blake
out the door.

"I'll text you in a while," Blake called as he drove away. Nicole
wanted to scream, but she stomped upstairs to call her sister
instead.

Life Story Questions

1. Put yourself in Blake's shoes. Thinking through the subject of this chapter, why might he have done what he did *without asking her*?

2. How does he view Nicole's questions and assumptions about his thought processes?

3. What could she have done differently? Should she? If she *did* do something differently, might it have an impact on what happens in the future?

Bringing It Home
Discussing It with Your Man

- Read the "Dadthink v. Momthink" story on pages 91–92 of *FWO*. Can you think of a time when I made certain assumptions about what you must have been thinking? Was I right or wrong? How did it make you feel?

- How am I doing in the area of giving you plenty of time and space for processing? Is there anything I could say or do to make it better for you in this area?

- As I learn, will you help me get this by pointing out when I'm rushing you for communication? What are some clues you could give me to let me know you need that time and space to think?

- Waiting to talk about something while you are processing it can be really painful for me. And I often *need* to talk it through. Is there a way we can set up a deadline when we'll talk, or is there some other way to give us both what we need?

The **Big** Idea

The one main idea I'm taking away from this week's discussion is:

The Loneliest Burden

How His Need to Provide Weighs Your Man Down, and Why He Likes It That Way

Even if you alone earned enough income to provide for your family, it would make no difference to the mental burden your husband feels to provide. Even for single men, being a provider is at the core of a man's identity. Men feel powerful when they provide, and providing is a way to express their love. Wives often get exasperated when husbands work late, which frustrates men because they think their long work hours (and the income that comes with them) are saying "I love you."

For this discussion: Read chapter 5 in the *FWO* book, and/or watch the second half of session 3 of the *FWO* video study.

Key Questions

1. What did you learn about men and their need to provide? How have you seen this played out in the relationships closest to you?

2. Give an example of a time when you may have added to a man's sense of provider burden or not appreciated the depth of it. Give an example of when you got it right.

3. How do you respond when your man works long hours? What can you do to alleviate the burden?

From the Video Study

One man said, "For a male, providing for the family is the most important thing that you do...from a security standpoint and providing things for the family. I would say it occupies 90 percent of my thought process and is the most important thing I do in getting recognition for that as a form of love."

Q What, to you, is the most startling part of this man's statement? Knowing that many men on the survey felt similarly, how does that make you feel about them?

Q Have you seen clues that men are looking for recognition that they provide as a form of love? What can you do to show that recognition?

Life Story

Blake has his own business providing audio and video services for conventions. He loves his work and is good at it, and over the years, he and Nicole have gotten used to the industry's seasonal fluctuations. However, during one particularly tight year, Nicole's mother and a friend began regularly expressing their concern about Blake's ability to safely take the family into retirement years. Nicole, always very practical, began subtly asking him to find a "real" job with benefits and a 401(k). Blake asked her to be patient, not to rush into a major change, and to trust that God would lead them. Nicole replied that God helps those who help themselves. Blake pointed out that that *wasn't* in the Bible, and increasingly the couple argued about the subject. Nicole felt torn between her desire to support her hard-working husband and her desire to follow the counsel of trusted others and nudge the family down a more practical financial path.

Life Story Questions

1. In this story, what did Nicole do well and not so well?

2. Put yourself in Blake's shoes. How do you think he is feeling about his ability to provide?

3. What might be some of the reasons he didn't want to find another job? List all possible emotional and physical reasons. Would understanding those things help Nicole?

4. What should Nicole do differently, if anything?

Bringing It Home
Discussing It with Your Man

- Give me an example of when you felt that I really understood the burden you feel to provide.
- Can you give me an example of when you felt that I didn't? How did that make you feel?
- How can I take some of the pressure off you? Would it be easier for you if we reduced our lifestyle? if I could bring in more income?
- [If the woman is the primary income earner] Is it difficult for you that I earn more money? Here's how I view that you are providing for the family:_____ (being a great husband, a great dad, and so on). How can I better show you how much I appreciate that?

The **Big** Idea

The one main idea I'm taking away from this week's discussion is:

Sex Changes Everything

Why Sex Unlocks a Man's Emotions (Guess Who Holds the Key?)

Your sexual desire for your husband profoundly affects his sense of well-being and confidence in all areas of his life. Men want to be wanted, and three out of four would still feel empty if their wives were not both sexually engaged and sexually satisfied. If this area is lacking, a man feels a deep sense of personal rejection and even depression. It usually takes an overt decision for a woman to get tuned in, involved, passionate, creative, and committed to ensuring that her husband feels desired by her. And for him, the feeling of closeness in the bedroom carries great weight when it comes to whether he feels close to her (and loved by her) outside the bedroom.

A note for singles: Although this subject focuses on marriage, it is still important to understand how men feel, as statistics indicate that most women will be married in their lifetime.

For this discussion: Read chapter 6 in the *For Women Only* book, and/or watch session 4 of the *For Women Only* video study.

Key Questions

1. Were you surprised about the men's responses in this chapter and the extreme *emotional* ramifications of sex—or the lack of it? If the emotional importance is true, what message does it send a man when his wife *initiates* sex?

2. What are some obstacles that may get in the way of a woman being an involved, passionate partner in intimacy? How can those be addressed?

3. Consider this quote on page 116 of *FWO:* "In making love, there is one other person in this world that you can be completely vulnerable with and be totally accepted and not judged. It is a solace that goes very deep into the heart of a man." If you are married, do you think your husband sees it that way? Does that change the way you view your husband's approaches? If you are single, what does this man's comment imply about how the men you know feel every day as they go through life?

 From the Video Study

One man says, "[Physical intimacy is] the glue that at times, even though it may feel like a chore, does so much for the man because that's the way we're wired, and that's when we feel the closest to our spouse."

Q Many men mentioned the idea of physical intimacy being
   the "glue" in the marriage. What do you think they mean by
   that?

Q Many men said that feeling of closeness carries over far beyond
   the bedroom. What evidence have you seen that men who have
   this need met feel closer to their spouses?

Q [If you are married] Does knowing this change how you look
   at physical intimacy in your marriage?

Life Story

During their first year of marriage, Nicole and Blake enjoyed the
physical intimacies of their new life together. During year two,
however, Nicole took a community-service position that she found
both exhilarating and demanding. Despite coming home ex-
hausted many evenings, she tried to make sure Blake knew she was
always (well, nearly always) sexually available, even if sometimes
she seemed to be going through the motions. As the months passed,
Nicole noticed that Blake began to seem somewhat withdrawn,
even despondent. When she asked him about it, he said that things
had changed. She used to be loving, available, adoring, and even
inviting; now she was someone else, he said. Her work and com-
munity relationships seemed to have stolen her away. And their sex

life just wasn't the same—some weeks the two were acting more like roommates than lovers. Blake's remarks confused Nicole. Yes, thinking back, she probably had been too tired to make love several times when he tried to initiate it, but she was doing everything she could to be a good wife. Didn't Blake understand that she was only one woman?

Life Story Questions

1. Make a list of the positive and negative messages Nicole was sending Blake.

2. Put yourself in Blake's shoes for a moment: Why was he becoming withdrawn and even despondent? What might the word *available* convey to him?

3. Is there a solution for this couple that meets both their needs?

Bringing It Home
Discussing It with Your Man

- If I am simply too tired or preoccupied to engage with you in intimacy, do you feel that I am rejecting *you*? If so, how can I communicate my inability to you without sending you that rejection message?

- Are there things I am doing for you that are tiring me out but are not, in your mind, as high a priority as this? If so, can you help me understand your priorities, and can we develop a plan to either eliminate or find another way to accomplish the other priorities?
- How do you most need to be loved in this area? What can I do to show my desire for you?
- What is your ideal frequency of sex? (Don't gasp at the answer.)
- Here are some needs I'd like to communicate in order for our love life to become more mutually satisfying.

--- The **Big** Idea ---

The one main idea I'm taking away from this week's discussion is:

Keeper of the Photo Files

Why It's So Difficult for Him Not to Look, and So Hard to Forget What He's Seen

Even happily married, devoted men are instinctively pulled to look at eye-magnet women, and most men have a set of mental photo files—almost like picture files on a computer—that can pop up in their thoughts without warning. As upsetting as these truths might be to some women, remember that temptation is not sin and your guy is likely trying his best to minimize those involuntary thoughts and win the battle of the mind. The lure doesn't happen because of you and has nothing to do with his feelings for you; in fact, most men wish they didn't have this temptation. As women, we can be supportive of our men's efforts to keep their thought lives pure, pray for them, champion modesty, and realize that God created men to be visual and that His creation is good.

For this discussion: Read chapter 7 in the *FWO* book, and/or watch session 5 of the *FWO* video study.

Key Questions

1. If it's true that men have a hard time not noticing "eye magnets" and that those images can later intrude upon their thoughts—even if they don't want them to—what is this culture like for our men?

2. What is the difference between temptation and sin?

3. How can we be supportive of men without in any way condoning or excusing inappropriate thoughts or actions?

From the Video Study

One man says, "I'm just making an observation that a man who wants to walk in godliness finds it difficult to do so with the distraction of certain fashions or certain styles of dress.… Why is it difficult? Because men are visual creatures."

Q Are you surprised or bothered that men feel this way—even godly men? What do you think this man means when he says walking in godliness can be difficult?

Q How can you support the guy you love as he faces a culture in which everyone is bombarded with visual images they were never supposed to see?

Life Story

After months of financial stress, Blake and Nicole were grateful when Blake began a lucrative two-month filming job for a producer of athletic gear, even though it meant he was out of town a lot. The video shoots were at a popular beach resort, and on the phone one night, Nicole joked to Blake that she wished she were "slaving away" in that environment too. Blake replied, "Actually, I wish you were here *instead* of me!" When Nicole asked what on earth he meant, he shut down and wouldn't explain. Three weeks into the high-paying job, Nicole was surprised when Blake said he was going to turn the job over to a female colleague. When she asked him why, she was both surprised and dismayed when he confessed that he was having a difficult time being around women with great athletic bodies in little bikinis all day and had begun being seriously tempted to turn on inappropriate movies in his hotel room at night. Nicole was devastated that Blake would have either temptation, and she began to wonder if she could trust him.

Life Story Questions

1. In what ways was Blake dishonoring his wife? In what ways was he honoring her?

2. How might Blake feel about his wife's reaction to his confession? How might he handle such a situation in the future, as a result?

3. How should Nicole handle her feeling of betrayal and the question of whether she can trust Blake?

Bringing It Home
Discussing It with Your Man

Author's note: Because this can be a difficult subject for husbands and wives to discuss, please approach it with discretion and compassion—including skipping the section if your husband prefers not to talk about it. For some couples, it will be better to discuss it with the help of a trained counselor.

- Can you help me understand what it is like when a very attractive woman appears in a man's line of sight? About how often do you get bombarded by eye magnets?

- The men in the research described images that pop up in their minds, almost like picture files on a computer. Since most female brains don't have an equivalent, help me understand how that works. Is there anything that makes images more likely to pop up in your mind, or is it random? How tough is it to erase or replace the images that surface? Is there anything I can do to help?

- Do you feel free to share your struggles or needs in this area with me? How can I best support you?

- In your opinion, how appropriately do I dress? Am I helping or hindering men with my clothing and tone?

The **Big** Idea

The one main idea I'm taking away from this week's discussion is:

Chocolate, Flowers, Bait Fishing

Why the Reluctant Romeo You Know Really Does Want Romance

Your man really does want romance, but he may think he has poor skills in this area. Or he may simply have different ideas about what is romantic. Most men would like more romance—yes, even apart from sex! Our men want connection, fun, and togetherness as much as we do. A guy views taking romantic initiative as a huge risk for humiliation or inadequacy, so you need to encourage him and prove that he's not at risk. Most men also view going out and doing things together as romantic.

For this discussion: Read chapter 8 in the *FWO* book, and/or watch most of session 6 of the *FWO* video study. (Important note: If you are doing this study in the order of the book chapters, not the video, stop the video before we explain the good-news conclusion. The last few minutes of the video are the conclusion to the entire *FWO* study, and you'll watch them with the last discussion in this guide.)

Key Questions

1. What surprised you about how men feel about romance?

2. Give an example of when you did something right in encouraging your man's attempts at romance. Give an example of when you may have inadvertently shut him down.

3. Consider this quote on page 172 of *FWO:* "A guy wants romance... to reexperience the spark of dating, to reconnect after days of draining work at the office, to feel love and intimacy, to know he is wanted and enjoyed, and to utterly escape the crushing nonstop pressure of life." Do you think the man in your life would agree? Does this change the way you view your responsibility in the area of romantic response?

From the Video Study

One man states, "I believe that men do like romance...just spending time together. Nothing superextravagant...just hanging out with the one that we love. Romance is more than just an elegant dinner out at a restaurant. It's more than just looking deeply into each other's eyes. Romance can be a baseball game sitting together on the couch in front of the TV."

Q   Are you surprised that a guy would define romance in this way? Do you think his example should count as romance? Why or why not?

Q   Looking back, do you think you may have missed certain signals that your man was trying to do something that he considered romantic?

Life Story

Blake didn't normally cook for the family, but he decided to surprise Nicole on their anniversary by arranging for the kids to stay with a baby-sitter and making her a romantic dinner. It was beautiful: china, candles, the works. The meal was lasagna, and it looked and smelled terrific. After a few bites, Nicole hopped up and got the salt, pepper, and oregano out of the cupboard. The couple had a nice evening, but in the following weeks Blake didn't respond to Nicole's hints that she'd love another dinner. It wasn't until months later that Blake admitted that he felt like his efforts had been judged to be inadequate that night and that it would be hard for him to attempt something like that again anytime soon.

Life Story Questions

1. What happened here? Why the hurt feelings from Blake? What might his sensitivity say about any areas of insecurity? Do you think his sensitivity is legitimate or that this shouldn't have bothered him?

2. What should Nicole have done differently that night, if anything?

3. Once Blake told her how he felt, how should she respond?

Bringing It Home
Discussing It with Your Man

- What do you view as romance? Is it a candlelight dinner? Just the two of us doing something? Give me some examples of what that might look like.
- What things do I do that encourage or discourage you from pursuing romance with me? If you want romance as I do, what can I do in the future to help?
- In your mind, is romance totally separate from sex? totally connected? Or is sex unconnected but a nice end to a romantic time together?

The **Big** Idea

The one main idea I'm taking away from this week's discussion is:

The Truth About Taking Care of Yourself

Why What's on the Outside Matters to Him on the Inside

What's on the outside (your appearance) matters to him on the inside. He doesn't need you to be a size 3, but he does want you to make an effort to take care of yourself for him. That makes him feel loved and helps him make the similarly difficult effort to keep his visual life pure. Men find this subject dangerous and can't honestly express their wishes because they don't want to hurt us (which is why this discussion has a different sort of "Bringing It Home" section). Men love our God-given individuality, sturdy thighs, small boobs, and all, and they wish we weren't so sensitive about our bodies; yet seven out of ten surveyed men said they would be emotionally bothered if their women let themselves go and didn't seem to care about making an effort to take care of themselves. Your man wants to feel proud of you, and he is totally willing to help you.

For this discussion: Read chapter 9 in the *FWO* book. (You can also watch the brief note about this again near the end of session 5 of the *FWO* video study.)

Key Questions

1. Is the desire of men in this area a legitimate one? Do you believe that if a husband truly loves his wife, then her lack of effort regarding her appearance shouldn't matter to him?

2. Do you think God cares about your effort regarding appearance? your energy? your health?

3. Does this subject make you cringe, anger you, or stir up another strong emotion? If so, why do you think that is the case?

From the Video Study

I quoted one man as saying, "If I see my wife making the effort to take care of herself for me, I feel like she cares about me. If she seems to not want to make the effort to take care of herself, I feel like she doesn't care about me."

Q Are you a woman who has thought that not making an effort only affected you? Do you think it is legitimate that many men feel otherwise?

Q What steps could you take to let the guy you love see you making that effort to care for his feelings in this area?

Life Story

After three kids and fifteen years of marriage, Nicole realized she had somehow put on twenty-five extra pounds and along the way had also quit wearing makeup and nice clothes, preferring sweatpants for hanging out. One day Blake joined a gym and started exercising and dieting. He never said a thing, but Nicole noticed that he became pensive if she brought a lot of junk food home from the store. They had a strong marriage, but things just didn't seem as fun between them anymore.

Life Story Questions

1. What was Blake trying to communicate?

2. Put yourself in Blake's shoes: Is there any way he can productively discuss his feelings with Nicole? (Does your answer suggest any options for your own marriage, if needed?)

3. What is Nicole's responsibility, if any?

Bringing It Home
Discussing It with Your Man

Unlike the other sessions, we strongly urge you not to talk to your man, but rather to do the following:

- Even without looking in the mirror or standing on a scale (as the book makes clear, this is not about weight; it applies to petite, size 3 women too!), ask yourself if you're really making an honest effort to take care of yourself for your husband.

- Ask a trusted, mature girlfriend to give you an honest, balanced appraisal and, if necessary, advice on changes you could make. This will also help ensure that you do not spiral out of control over issues that really aren't issues!

- Pray about all this until you have peace.

The **Big** Idea

The one main idea I'm taking away from this week's discussion is:

Words for Your Heart

What Your Man Most Wishes You Knew About Him

What surveyed men most wished to convey to women was not how much we could improve our appearance or which of our attitudes needed adjustment or how to better our performance in the relationship...but how much they love us! One man said, "It is so true that behind every great man is a great woman. There are a lot of men out there who are mediocre, simply because their wives will not support them and bring them to greatness. And there are a lot of mediocre men who are destined to become great men—who are becoming great men—because their wives love and support them."

For this discussion: Read chapter 10 in the *FWO* book, and/or watch the end of session 6 of the *FWO* video study.

Key Questions

1. How does the man's comment (above) make you feel?

2. In what ways that you may not even recognize might your man be trying to express or show his love? How do you respond? How *should* you respond?

3. If you have children, how are you training them now to become the kind of husbands or wives they'll need to be in the future?

From the Video Study

I quote a well-known pastor: "I know you all think you've got a good pastor. I know you all think that. You don't. You've got a great pastor's wife."

Q Are you smiling and sighing with me over this comment? Why? What does this stir up in you?

Q Does it make you want to be that type of woman? What one thing can you do differently, if anything, to be the wife (or girlfriend or mom or...) that God has called you to be?

A Final Challenge

- To keep you on a great path in your relationship, I encourage you to glance back through this guide and identify two or three specific application steps you want to continue working on over the next several weeks:

    1.

    2.

    3.

- Affirm the For Women Only Covenant on page 51, either individually or as a group, then cut it out and post it. Use the list as a handy reference to jog your memory in the future.

Remember, the man in your life already loves you. And now you have also gained some fantastic skills and knowledge to be able to show him just how you feel about him too.

Bringing It Home
Discussing It with Your Man

- Have you ever tried to convey your love for me but ended up feeling like I didn't really believe you?
- Is there anything that I say or do that encourages you in your expressions of love? discourages you?
- Here is a unique way you make me feel loved:

    _____.

- I want to support you in becoming all God intends you to become. Based on my new understanding of you, what one thing can I commit to do that would most make you feel supported going forward?

The **Big** Idea

The one main idea I'm taking away from this week's discussion is:

The For Women Only Covenant

Now that my eyes have been opened to my man's inner life, I will…

1. Assume the best about him as a man made in God's image and do my part to understand his unique desires and needs.

2. Choose to trust him and join the adventure, even when he's driving in circles and won't ask for directions.

3. Catch myself before I complain about him to others—and brag about him instead.

4. Every day find something he's really good at and then affirm him in that area.

5. Give him the time he needs to process things, believing that he wants to communicate well with me.

6. Notice how he feels about providing and thank him for his commitment.

7. Recognize that my husband doesn't just want more sex but also needs to feel that I desire and enjoy him sexually.

8. Pray daily for him in our visually distracting culture, and support and appreciate his efforts to keep his thought life pure.

9. Understand that he may be proposing a romantic rendezvous when he says, "Hey, honey—wanna go to Home Depot with me?"

10. Make sure he sees me making an effort to take care of myself for him.

11. Embrace his efforts to tell me how much he loves me—in whatever way he conveys that best—and let him know that I believe him.

Guide 2

For Men Only

Discussion Guide

Shaunti and Jeff Feldhahn with Brian Smith

Guide 2 Contents

How to Use the *For Men Only Discussion Guide*

I (Jeff) imagine you've picked up this book in search of some help navigating the wild, seemingly unpredictable inner world of women. Or—let's be frank—because the woman in your life "strongly suggested" that you needed such help.

Hmm.

Most of us genuinely want to be better husbands, boyfriends, or fathers; we simply need a little help in figuring out how. And that's the basic idea behind this guide: using the insights from the *For Men Only* book and video study to identify simple changes that can make huge differences in our relationships.

How to Use This Guide

I hope you'll find this guide helpful whether you're married, dating, or single. You'll see that I use the words *woman, wife,* and *girlfriend* somewhat interchangeably. (The only exception is that I use *wife* when discussing sex, since I agree with the biblical principle of reserving physical intimacy for marriage.) My main goal is to help you apply these ideas in your romantic relationship, but I think you'll find they will also help you relate better to other women in your life, like your daughter, female coworker, or friend. You can explore this guide on your own or use it as the map for a discussion group. And you can use it with the *FMO* book, video study, or both. (Note: I will use *FMO* to mean *For Men Only* throughout this guide.)

Note that the different discussion elements and questions are designed to be mixed and matched; pick and choose what works for you and your group to help get us oh-so-sensitive men talking.

Speaking of being a sensitive man, you'll also see a section called "On the Home Front" at the end of each group-discussion section. It gives you conversation starters to use with your woman privately later. Chances are, all you'll need to do is ask a question or two and she'll gladly take it from there.

Are You Using Just the Book? Video Study? Both?

You can use this guide with either the book or the video study. Or you can use both together—which is sure to be the greatest help in understanding the perplexing woman in your life. (Did I say *perplexing*? I meant *extraordinary*.) Here are a few guidelines.

If You Are Using Just the Book

Each session in this guide corresponds to a chapter in the *FMO* book (the updated 2013 edition), and it is laid out in the same order as the book. Thus, chapter 2 in this guide corresponds to chapter 2 in the book. (You can bribe your leader to start with chapter 7 if you want.)

If You Are Going Through the Video Study

The *For Men Only* video study is organized in six ten-to-twelve-minute segments. Each video includes about two minutes of interviews with women explaining how they think. If you're pressed for time, simply skip those interviews. The order of the video subjects is different from the book order, as the subjects were combined in some cases. So if you're doing the video study, you will follow this order:

Video	FMO Book and Guide
Session 1: Decoding	Chapter 4
Session 2: Reassurance	Chapter 2
Session 3: Security / Listening	Chapter 5 / Chapter 6
Session 4: Sex	Chapter 7
Session 5: Beauty	Chapter 8
Session 6: Emotions (Windows) / Good News	Chapter 3 / Chapter 9

If You Are Using Both the Book and the Videos

You can use the book as the primary resource, with the video as a supplement, or vice versa; you'll just need to decide which order you are going to follow.

A note to group leaders: At the beginning of each of the studies in this guide, we indicate which video session and book chapter are covered in that lesson. As noted, several of the video sessions cover multiple topics. So if you are doing this study in the order of the book chapters, not the video sessions, pay attention to what part of the video you are directed to watch so you don't give away the surprise by playing a part of a video that corresponds to a different subject.

Yes, This Guide Is Biased

Sometimes, as you work and talk through the book and guide, you may feel that you're being treated unfairly. "It seems like all the responsibility is on me," I can hear you groan. "Where's equal time for her to learn about *my* needs?" Well, all that's covered in another book called *For Women Only* and its companion video and discussion guide. (If you want to take a peek at what we're saying about you, check the first guide in this 3-in-1 resource.)

For our purposes, though, I've kept this discussion guide focused on what you need to know in order to understand the inner workings of that enigma called *woman*. It's not supposed to help you change her; rather, it is supposed to help you change and improve yourself. Which is why at the end of this *FMO* study (pages 88–90), I suggest you allot a few minutes to think through and fill out the Final Challenge section to decide what you will commit to working on going forward, as well as a list of resolutions you can make on your own or with the other members of your group. I've seen firsthand that applying these simple truths will result in incalculable benefits for *both* of you.

The Deal Is Never Closed

Why Her "I Do" Will Always Mean "Do You?"—and What to Do About It

Even if your relationship is great, your mate likely has a fundamental insecurity about your love. Her feelings of insecurity are surprisingly frequent, intensely painful, and—to the male mind—paradoxically resistant to logic. When her insecurity is triggered by conflict between you or your withdrawal, she may respond in ways that confuse or dismay you. But when you're clued in, those puzzling behaviors serve as red warning lights signaling you to respond to her need by verbally reassuring her of your love and by actively pursuing her to show that you would choose her all over again.

For this discussion: Read chapter 2 in the *FMO* book, and/or watch session 2 of the *FMO* video study.

Key Questions

1. What signals might your wife or girlfriend be sending that would indicate she's feeling insecure about your love? Play detective: What words or body language might communicate her need?

2. Describe an instance when your wife needed to be reassured of your love but you missed the opportunity. Contrast the outcome of that scenario with a time you recognized her need and responded well.

3. What words or actions have worked best for you in reassuring and pursuing your wife or girlfriend? (Everyone, take notes. This'll be good stuff to try.)

From the Video Study

Shaunti said, "There is no switch in a woman's brain that gets flipped to the 'I feel permanently loved' position. Instead, either as a conscious question or running under the surface is *Would he choose me all over again?* She needs to know every single day that you would choose her all over again. But the problem starts when she doesn't know that."

Q Do you feel like the woman in your life "should" know that you love her, even if you don't tell her? If so, why do you feel that way?

Q Compare her need for reassurance of your love to our need to feel reassured by a boss that we're doing a good job. Does this comparison make her desire for reassurance seem more legitimate? What can/should we do as a result?

On the Home Front

Discussing It with Her

- I didn't realize that you might sometimes wonder whether I really love you. Just for the record, I do! What are some situations or things I might say or do that make you worry about us or about whether I truly love you?
- What are a few of the things I say and do that most make you feel reassured that I do love you and will always be here for you?
- When we're arguing or frustrated with each other, how can I reassure you of my love while still giving myself time to process what's happening?

The **Big** Idea

The one main idea I'm taking away from this week's discussion is:

Windows...Open!

What You Should Know About the Fabulous Female Brain

Men generally focus on one thing at a time, compartmentalizing other thoughts and feelings for later consideration. But most women experience multiple thoughts and emotions at the same time that can't easily be dismissed. Many women are blindsided regularly by negative, unresolved thoughts and feelings from the recent or far past. Sudden shifts in topic, introduction of "ancient history," or flashes of emotion often signal a past or current concern that keeps invading a woman's awareness even if she doesn't want it there. These concerns are like pop-up windows on a computer, and you can help close those windows by nondefensively allowing her to talk out and/or resolve whatever concern is popping up. You might even take some action to resolve it for her.

For this discussion: Read chapter 3 in the *FMO* book, and/or watch the first part of session 6 of the *FMO* video study. (Important note: If you are doing this study in the order of the book chapters, not the order of the video sessions, *stop the video before we explain the good-news conclusion.* The last few minutes of the video are the powerful—dare I say *emotional?*—conclusion to the entire *FMO* study, and you'll see them when you do the last session in this guide.)

Key Questions

1. Think of something your wife or girlfriend has said or done that sent you spinning at the time but that now makes more sense in light of this chapter. How did you respond then? If you were given a do-over (don't you wish!), what would you do differently in light of your newfound understanding?

2. In your own experience, what other evidence have you seen that women are constantly juggling multiple thoughts and feelings and can't always close those that are bothering them?

3. Describe a typical situation in which the woman you love might have trouble closing a particular mental window. The next time this occurs, how could you step up to help her resolve her concerns and close the window? (Hint: "Rebooting her" is not a valid answer.)

From the Video Study

One woman says, "We have this huge ball of string in our head. Everything here is connected. We can't shut something off and [just] go to this one or go to that one. Men compartmentalize, [but] we don't do that."

Q Imagine for a moment (we promise, only a moment) that your thoughts are like a ball of string with no end point and there's no easy way to shut them off. Now imagine that something is worrying you. What is the natural progression of that worry?

Q   Since she can't take a giant pair of scissors and cut the string to end that worry, what does she want and need in order to feel better?

On the Home Front
Discussing It with Her

- Is it true that women tend to have many things running through their minds, all at the same time? What's in your brain right now?
- When you mention a concern to me and I respond with "Just don't worry about it," what usually happens in your mind? Are you able to push that concern aside? How would you prefer I respond in that situation?

—— The **Big** Idea ——

The one main idea I'm taking away from this week's discussion is:

The Reason Hiding in Her "Unreasonable" Reaction

How You Can Actually Break the Code of Baffling Female Behavior

Starting in our teen years, we assume that either (1) there is no rhyme or reason behind a girl's reactions, or (2) if there is a reason, we'll never be able to understand it. We throw up our hands, try to ignore the problem, or just leave her alone and hope things will calm down on their own—all of which tend to make things worse. We would never ignore a sudden whine in the gears of a favorite car and hope it gets better on its own; why do we do that with her? Well, with a car, we assume there is a reason for the whine that can be addressed and if we look closely we'll find it. Amazingly, it's the same thing with women. If she's doing something confusing, it is rooted in a specific reason that we can figure out. Even more important—sort of like the whine in the gearshift—those "out of nowhere" behaviors are often specific signals of a need we are being asked to meet.

For this discussion: Read chapter 4 in the *FMO* book, and/or watch session 1 of the *FMO* video study.

Key Questions

1. If your woman ever has seemed random or confusing, describe an example. How did you handle it? Did you duck out in confusion, stick with it to figure out what was really going on, or a little of both? What was her reaction to your choice?

2. Have you ever been in a situation where you assumed she was just being random but later realized there was a reason? What did you do about it when you found out the reason? What could you do better next time?

3. How tough is it to assume there's a legitimate reason behind her actions and to continue to stay engaged and try to find an answer—without getting defensive or withdrawing? What specific things will help you stay in the game, knowing it's worth it to preserve the relationship? What are some key ways a man can play detective and find the reason for the randomness?

From the Video Study

One woman said, "Sometimes my husband might see that I'm quiet or sitting somewhere in a corner and I'm really not talking. And he might think, *Oh, she just wants to sit there,* but there's a reason why, and if he'll just sit down and ask me, or look a little deeper, he might actually realize that there's something going on with me."

Q What keeps us from looking a little deeper when a woman looks distant, worried, or moody? Make a list of at least three different reasons.

Q If looking deeper is really what they need from us, how can we overcome each of the roadblocks you listed?

On the Home Front
Discussing It with Her

Just in case you were wondering, the best time to ask these questions is *not* when you're totally confused. But I guarantee that at any other time, they will start a highly informative discussion.

- There are times I just don't understand why you are reacting in a certain way and what you need from me. But I want you to know how much I love you. What can help us overcome that confusion? If I'm confused, should I tell you I'm confused? Or would that hurt your feelings?

- Can you give me an example of a time you said something like "I'm fine" when you weren't fine and needed me to dig deeper into how you were feeling—but I withdrew instead?

What specifically would you have wanted me to do instead?
(I promise not to get defensive this time.)

- Do you ever hold back from sharing what you're thinking,
or from telling me a concern, because you think I will get
defensive or overreact? Here is a way you could say it that
would help me receive it well, instead of as criticism (for
example, "Start with affirmation, then share the concern"):

_____.

The **Big** Idea

The one main idea I'm taking away from this week's discussion is:

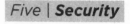

Your Real Job Is Closer to Home

How Your Provider/Protector Instinct Can Leave Her Feeling More Unsafe and Less Cared For

While most men think that a woman wants financial security, what most women want even more is emotional security. That is, she wants to feel close to you, to know that she's your non-work-time priority, to know you're committed to her, and to have you involved at home. And although she does want financial security, wants you to be fulfilled in your work, and appreciates your efforts to provide, she'd willingly endure financial struggles if that's what it took to have more of you (such as if you wanted a lower-paying, more family-friendly job). Fortunately, building emotional security and closeness is easier than you might think. Making small gestures of love and spending discretionary hours with her and at home instead of working overtime will go a long way.

For this discussion: Read chapter 5 in the *FMO* book, and/or watch the security part of session 3 of the *FMO* video study.

Key Questions

1. Describe a situation in which your wife or girlfriend is most likely to complain that she doesn't get enough of you. What underlying issue or circumstance seems to provoke this comment most often?

2. If she were able to converse in Man-Talk (Manglish? Mannese? Mandarin?), how might she express her desire in a way that made sense to you?

3. What actions or words on your part seem to satisfy her need for connection? How can you tell those efforts are successful? Do they have to be exhausting and difficult to do in order to be effective?

From the Video Study

I quote a guy who said, "Oh sure, women say [they prefer emotional security] when things are going okay. But let's just see what they say once things go south for a while!" We explained, "But then we looked at the demographics, and the women who identified themselves as being in the most desperate situations financially were even *more* likely to say they preferred closeness and emotional security!"

Q Why do we as guys find this so hard to believe?

Q If all this is true, what are the implications for us? If our presence
and closeness actually are more important than the stuff, what
specifically should we do differently in the short term? long term?

On the Home Front
Discussing It with Her

- Do you ever wonder if my work is more important to me
  than you are?
- What are some things I already do that let you know you're
  a priority in my life? What other little things could I do to
  help you feel loved and secure?
- What are your nonnegotiables when it comes to our
  financial or material needs? What are your nonnegotiables
  in our relationship?

The **Big** Idea

The one main idea I'm taking away from this week's discussion is:

Listening *Is* the Solution

Why Her Feeling About the Problem Is the Problem and How to Fix Your Urge to Fix

When a woman voices an emotional concern, our first instinct is to set aside her emotions, identify the technical problem, and fix it. But what she needs first is for you to give her your full attention, set aside the technical problem, and instead listen to and validate what she's feeling about it…as odd as that feels. By restating her concern and telling her it's okay to feel that way, you will actually fix a problem for her—the emotional one that needs to be addressed before she will be interested in actually tackling the technical one. As you learn to listen in the way she needs, you may sometimes feel that she's blaming you when in fact she probably appreciates you more than you realize.

For this discussion: Read chapter 6 in the *FMO* book, and/or watch the "listening" part of session 3 of the *FMO* video study again.

Key Questions

1. Are you often surprised by negative responses when you offer solutions to your wife's or girlfriend's concerns without first

acknowledging her feelings? Describe a time you thought you were being helpful but your wife or girlfriend accused you of not listening or caring. What response do you think she was looking for?

2. What distractions most often compete for your attention when your wife or girlfriend wants to talk? What's your new strategy for giving her your full attention?

3. Those four little words—"We need to talk"—can instantly drain our energy, even before the conversation begins. How could you let her know about your listening limitations and how working within those constraints might help your relationship?

From the Video Study

I explained, "She can figure out a solution on her own if she has to, but she can't feel listened to on her own. The key is to listen to her *feelings*— her worries, her hurts, her excitement, her fear. And listening in that way truly does help solve the problem, the real problem, because you're helping her work through all those jangling emotions. And *that* is what makes them really feel heard. The women told me that this really is a secret weapon for a guy to build a great sense of closeness between them."

Q Why is it that we automatically want to jump to a solution without listening to her feelings?

Q Why does it feel like listening to her feelings isn't the same as doing something? Does good listening, in fact, involve doing something?

Q What are some effective strategies that will help us stop ourselves from jumping into a fix (pun intended!) *before* we listen to her feelings?

On the Home Front
Discussing It with Her

- I'm trying to learn how to listen in the way you need me to. Can you give me an example of a time you shared something with me and felt I was more focused on fixing than on listening?
- I realize that when you want to talk about issues in our relationship, sometimes I get kind of defensive, feeling like I'm always the one at fault. Am I jumping to conclusions, or is this really how you feel?
- What kind of signals should I watch for to know when you want me to help solve a problem versus when you just need me to hear out your feelings?

The **Big** Idea

The one main idea I'm taking away from this week's discussion is:

With Sex, Her "No" Doesn't Mean You

How Her Desires Are Impacted by Her Unique Wiring and Why Your Ego Shouldn't Be

Most women tend to crave sex less often than men do, and it's usually not because the woman doesn't desire her husband. A woman's sexual wiring is distinctly different from a man's, with a different hormone mix, a more emotional (instead of visual) orientation, and a physical and mental need for anticipation time. Often she's as frustrated as you are by the sexual differences between you and would change those factors if she could. The good news is, just a few simple changes can propel you toward the kind of sexual relationship both of you want. These include building the day-to-day closeness she needs outside the bedroom, flirting with her (again, outside the bedroom) so she knows she's attractive and desirable and you'd choose her all over again, and letting her know what's on your menu for the evening well before you step into the bedroom.

For this discussion: Read chapter 7 in the *FMO* book, and/or watch session 4 of the *FMO* video study.

Key Questions

1. What's the most helpful insight you gained from this chapter about the physical aspects of a woman's sexual wiring? What about the emotional aspects?

2. On a typical day, how would you describe your wife's attitude toward sex? How does this compare with her attitude once you're engaged in the act? What do you think explains this?

3. Think about one time when you knew your wife was really into it. You felt that she found you deeply desirable and expressed it through sex. What, if anything, did you say or do that helped lead to this outcome? What other circumstances might have contributed to her increased interest?

 From the Video Study

One woman explains, "[Men] think, *If you were really interested, you would be interested now.* We're not wired that way. We don't have those thoughts every eight seconds like you do. It's not how we're wired and how we're made, and we have to be physically charged and ready. If we're emotionally drained, it's just difficult, and sometimes almost impossible, to make that connection. [What should you do about it? Well, just knowing in advance helps.] A good example is the flirting and just building up during the day and then a phone call at lunch or a text to say, 'Hey, I'm really looking forward to tonight.' That builds you up and then you're ready to have that relationship and be intimate."

Q Does the idea of giving her anticipation time feel awkward and as if you have to give her advance notice (that is, warn her)? Where does the idea that you *shouldn't* have to give advance notice come from?

Q If this really is important to her, what are some ways you can do it that feel natural to you?

On the Home Front
Discussing It with Her

- If I don't bring it up, do you think about sex during the day? How often do you think about wanting sex if I haven't put the thought in your head or if it's not our "usual" time? (Fair warning: The typical answer may be hard to hear, like "Uh, never.")

- Does it make a difference in your emotional or physical interest level if you have some time to anticipate and start thinking about our being intimate? What suggestions do you have for how I could give you advance notice of how I'd love the evening to end—without making you feel like I was demanding something?

- Most of us guys want to be intimate with our wives in order to feel closer, but I understand that most women want and need to feel close before they will be interested in sex. Do you feel that we need to build more closeness outside the bedroom? Can you give me some examples of what I do during the day that helps lay that foundation of feeling close? What else can I do to help us build that closeness?

The **Big** Idea

The one main idea I'm taking away from this week's discussion is:

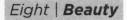

The Girl in the Mirror

What the Little Girl Inside Your Woman Is Dying to Hear from You—and How to Guard Your Answer Well

A woman is unlikely to outgrow the little-girl need to hear that you—the man in her life—find her beautiful. She's bombarded daily with demeaning images and messages, and she has a deeply rooted need to be reassured. You can counteract negative internal dialogue and external pressure by frequently and sincerely telling her she's beautiful to you, budgeting for her efforts to feel beautiful, and deliberately avoiding the impulse to let your eyes or thoughts dwell on other women.

For this discussion: Read chapter 8 in the *FMO* book, and/or watch session 5 of the *FMO* video study.

Key Questions

1. What's a typical way your wife or girlfriend might fish for your affirmation of her beauty? (If your answer is "I have no idea what you're talking about," please stop and ask the group for immediate

prayer.) What kinds of responses have you given that seem to meet her hunger for affirmation? What kinds of responses have backfired?

2. One of these days she's sure to ask your opinion about her appearance, and it's going to be one of the scary questions about some aspect you don't find quite so beautiful. How might you both affirm her and support her efforts at improvement—without digging yourself into a hole?

3. You know how much it would hurt your wife or girlfriend if you cheated on her sexually. Now consider Jesus's teaching: "Anyone who even looks at a woman with lust has already committed adultery with her in his heart" (Matthew 5:28). What steps can you take to guard against lustful eyes or thoughts?

 From the Video Study

I explain, "Even if it feels artificial, it matters to her when you send a text message from work saying, 'Have I told you today you're beautiful?' Now, it has to be something authentic to you—but *say* it. And the habit will be built."

Q Is one reason you don't tell her that you find her beautiful because you just don't realize how important it is for your woman to know it? Or does saying it at random times feel artificial—and surely she'll think you're not really being sincere? Should that keep us from doing it?

Q What are some simple ways you can convey to the woman you love just how beautiful she is to you—ways that can become a habit for you?

On the Home Front
Discussing It with Her

- Have I told you today how absolutely gorgeous you are? Do you have any idea how glad I am that you're mine?
- Did you know that one of the things I love most about you is _____?
- What can I do (or do I do) that lets you know that regularly?

Note: Our primary focus in this section was on a woman's need to know she's beautiful. But there is another point that some of us need to deal with as well. Telling her that she's beautiful becomes meaningless if she feels—or knows—that she's in competition with other women for your attention.

Let's be real. Keeping your eyes only for her isn't easy, but the results of giving in to temptation are devastating for both of you. If you're struggling with lust or pornography, I urge you to not brush it off as unimportant or deceive yourself into thinking it will go away. Please check out the many specialized resources available to help you, and perhaps even guide you through a serious conversation with your wife, if necessary. You might want to start at www.pureintimacy.org.

The **Big** Idea

The one main idea I'm taking away from this week's discussion is:

The Man She Had Hoped to Marry

What the Woman Who Loves You Most, Most Wants You to Know

Beneath all the differences, the miscommunications, the frustrations, nearly all women wish their husbands knew one basic truth: they deeply need, desire, and respect their men. Your wife or significant other doesn't always know how to show it, but it is very likely she always feels it. In her eyes, you are the hero she had hoped to marry. The woman you love honestly loves and admires you. And you have what it takes to be the leader, protector, friend, and support she needs you to be.

For this discussion: Read chapter 9 in the *FMO* book, and/or watch the last few minutes of session 6 of the *FMO* video study.

Key Questions

1. When you stop and think about it, what signs do you see in your wife's or girlfriend's words and actions that she *does* need and respect you?

2. Aside from being an irresistibly studly hunk, what have you done to earn her admiration? What do you think she would describe as your greatest assets as her provider, protector, husband, and friend? Where do you think you can improve?

3. Let's say you suspect you're among the very small percentage of men whose wives truly are unhappy. What steps can you take to improve your relationship?

From the Video Study

In this session we say, "We gave the women an open-ended question: 'What's the one most important thing you wish your husband or boyfriend knew but you feel he doesn't understand?' And instead of a laundry list of complaints, the top answer by far was 'I wish he understood that he is my hero...that he is the guy I hoped he would be when we married...that the average guy who leaves his fly down and the toilet seat up really is my knight in shining armor.'"

Q Does it surprise you to hear that your wife probably thinks you're an amazing guy and that she isn't spending her day wishing you were someone you weren't?

Q How might having that confidence in how she really feels about you change how you interact with her? For example, does it diminish your self-doubt about pleasing her, and might that make you less defensive when she says something that frustrates you?

A Final Challenge (and On the Home Front)

- To propel you further down the road to relational bliss (or at least prevent you from wandering back into the swamp), I encourage you to glance back through this guide and identify two or three specific application steps you want to continue working on over the next several weeks:

  1.

  2.

  3.

- Make the For Men Only Resolutions on the next two pages, either individually or as a group. Use them as a handy reference to jog your memory in the future.

Remember, you're already her hero. And now you have also gained some fantastic skills and knowledge that many guys never grasp. You have the map to her heart. Be encouraged as you continue on the adventure with her with confidence.

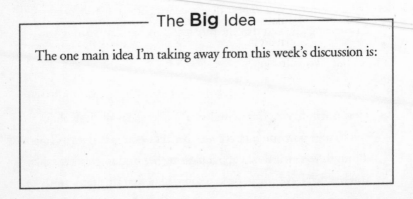

— The **Big** Idea —

The one main idea I'm taking away from this week's discussion is:

The For Men Only Resolutions

Now that I better understand the inner life of the woman I love, I will...

1. Assume that her reactions are a natural, logical part of her uniquely feminine nature and will do my part to ensure that she feels understood and loved.

2. Frequently reassure her of my love and commitment, even when her insecurity is not my fault.

3. Continue to pursue her in big ways and little ways—a touch, a note, an occasional mushy compliment—even though I've already caught her.

4. Try not to take it personally when she brings up something old, emotional, or off topic that I think she should be able to just let go; instead, I will encourage her to talk it out and resolve it...or maybe even take action that will resolve it for her.

5. Realize that providing means lots of things besides money, bring my work hours in line with our shared priorities, and devote the first share of my off-work hours to connecting with her and helping out at home.

6. Set aside the obvious problem—work frustrations, misbehaving kids, manipulative relatives—when she voices an emotional concern and then address the real issue by listening to, acknowledging, and affirming her feelings.

7. Try not to take offense when she says no to sex and understand that it's probably not about me but about her sexual wiring.

8. Show her affection in nonsexual ways every day, give her time to warm up to the idea of sex, and do my best to help her get full

satisfaction from sex. (Okay, I'll brush my teeth and take a shower too.)

9. Tell her often that she's the most exciting, attractive woman in the world to me and prove it by reserving my eyes only for her.

10. Believe that she respects and admires me, even if she doesn't always show it, and continue to work to be worthy of it.

Guide 3

For Couples Only

Discussion Guide

Shaunti and Jeff Feldhahn with Lisa A. Rice

Guide 3 Contents

How to Use the *For Couples Only* Discussion Guide

Greetings! We're glad you joined us to investigate the mysterious inner workings of your mate. We have based this study on the sweet spot that we've found works best for *couples'* purposes over the years. Most important is that men and women hear and discuss everything together. In this study, you will frequently find questions specific to either women or men, but that doesn't mean men or women should go off into separate rooms and talk. Much the reverse, in fact: these questions are designed so the "other half" can hear and learn from what is being shared.

Designed for All Uses

This study is purposefully designed to be very flexible. It can be used with the *For Couples Only* video teaching, with the books (*For Women Only* and *For Men Only*), or with both. It can be used in a group setting (such as a Sunday school class, small group, or book club) or by a couple alone (such as in premarital counseling, marriage mentoring, counseling, or just for fun). At the end of each group-discussion section, there is a "Bringing It Home" section to facilitate a private conversation between you and your mate.

Each of the six sessions is made up of two parts—a part 1 ("Understanding Men") and a part 2 ("Understanding Women"). If your group is meeting for six weeks, you will want to complete both part 1 and part 2 for each session, watching the video for both parts one after the other and then choosing and discussing the corresponding questions for both.

If your group is meeting for twelve weeks, you could choose to do part 1 of a session one week (including the part 1 discussion questions) and then part 2 and its discussion-questions the following week.

All the group-discussion questions and case studies are designed to be mixed and matched. Since you will not get through all of them in one session (especially if you're doing this over six weeks and thus are covering both a man's subject and a woman's subject each time), you should pick and choose which key questions and/or case studies work best for your group and the time you have available.

If You Are Using the Video Study

The *For Couples Only Discussion Guide* will be most effective when used with the video (whether or not you are also reading the books), since it is arranged in the order of the video sessions. The order of the video sessions is different from the order of the books' chapters.

Just like this discussion guide, each of the six video teaching sessions is made up of two parts—a part 1 ("Understanding Men") and a part 2 ("Understanding Women"). Each of these twelve video segments is ten to twelve minutes long. (Each part includes two to three minutes of interviews with men and women explaining how they think. If you are pressed for time, simply skip these interviews. Note that there is also a five-minute introduction that appears at the beginning of session 1.)

If You Are Using the Books and Not the Video

Each of the six sessions in this discussion guide uses a chapter from both *For Women Only* and *For Men Only*. Since this guide is in the order of the videos, not the books' chapters, we recommend reading through the chapters and discussing them in the order specified in this guide. Both men and women should read the relevant chapters from *both* books if possible. (It is just as helpful to learn what the other person doesn't know about you!)

If You Are Using Both the Books and Video

This is the ideal way to use this guide to get the most perspective. But don't worry; regardless of which method you choose, there is a note at the beginning of each part of each discussion section that will direct you to the appropriate videos and book chapters.

A Note to Group Leaders

At the end of the study, please be sure to allow the couples a few minutes to discuss the "Going Forward with Your Mate" question on page 151.

Also, a group leader's guide can be found in the "Studies" section of our website, www.jeffandshaunti.com. Other resources for group leaders (including bonus interview footage not included on the DVDs) can also be found there.

So are you ready to get started? Let's turn to session 1 and begin investigating the innermost feelings of the person sitting next to you.

Part 1: Understanding Men

Insecurity

The Performance of a Lifetime

Despite their in-control exteriors, men often feel like impostors and are insecure because they fear that their inadequacies will be discovered. Men believe they're being watched and judged constantly, and three out of four men surveyed admit to feigning competency despite feelings of inadequacy. Yet the "conquering" part of men loves the challenge. The key for a woman is to constantly affirm her man and create a safety zone at home.

For this discussion, both men and women should read chapter 3 in the *For Women Only* book and/or watch session 1, part 1 of the *For Couples Only* video study.

Key Questions

1. Share some examples of when you have observed a man who was acting confident but was probably hiding the vulnerability inside. (Men: Feel free to share some examples in your own life, if you wish.)

2. Men: What is the best way for a woman to respond to this sense of self-doubt? In particular, what should she *avoid* and what should she *do?* Does this mean walking on eggshells? Or is there another way of looking at this?

3. What is the best way for a man to handle or respond to his own sense of self-doubt?

4. In particular, when a woman hits that nerve, how can or should a man respond in a way that makes the situation better instead of worse?

Case Study

Barb and Grant were dining with some friends at a restaurant when the subject of future goals came up. Grant surprised everyone (including his wife) with the announcement that he was picking his guitar up again and that he and his old band friends had been thinking about jamming together on a weekly basis. Grant mentioned that he hoped they'd be booked for gigs in the city and how cool it would be to finally be able to transition to doing music as a career someday. Barb's jaw dropped open, and then she blurted, "Guess I won't be quitting my day job for a while!" The others laughed, and Grant changed the subject quickly.

Case Study Questions

1. Women: What do you think Grant was thinking as he made this announcement in this way? What do you think Grant was thinking and feeling when Barb said what she did?

2. Men: What do you think Grant was thinking as he made this announcement this way? What do you think Grant was thinking and feeling when Barb said what she did?

3. What could each have done differently? *Should* they have done that?

Bringing It Home

Discussing It Privately with Him

- What is it that I do that makes you feel like I'm saying "You're inadequate"?
- What is it that I do that makes you feel like you're doing a good job as a husband (or boyfriend), father, provider, and romancer?
- What can I do to build you up to be the man you want to be?

My **Notes**

Part 2: Understanding Women

Decoding

The Reason Hiding in Her "Unreasonable" Reaction

Starting in our teen years, guys assume that either (1) there is no rhyme or reason behind a girl's reactions, or (2) if there is a reason, they'll never be able to understand it. They throw up their hands, try to ignore the problem, or just leave her alone and hope things will calm down on their own—all of which tend to make things worse. The key for men is to assume, instead, that just like when something confusing happens on his computer, something confusing about his woman is rooted in a specific reason. And he can figure out that reason and see that those "out of nowhere" behaviors are often specific signals of a need she is asking him to meet.

For this discussion, both men and women should read chapter 4 in the *For Men Only* book and/or watch session 1, part 2 of the *For Couples Only* video study.

Key Questions

1. Men: Have you ever seen what seemed like randomness at work? Or can you think of a case where a guy thought *That came out of nowhere* or *I cannot figure her out*? Give some examples.

2. What are some key ways a man can play detective and find the reason for the randomness? What could a woman do to make it easier for a man to play detective and decode what is going on?

3. How can a woman share a concern in a way that her man will receive it well, instead of as criticism?

Case Study

Abbie and Trevor had been dating for the two years since they graduated from college. Trevor decided to celebrate the anniversary by taking Abbie out to a very high-end restaurant. After years of part-time and entry-level jobs, Trevor had gotten a major promotion, and there was a little extra money in the bank for the first time. Over dinner, Abbie tentatively brought up the subject of where their relationship was heading. She had mentioned something similar a few months before, but Trevor was a bit uncomfortable discussing it. He would rather show his love for her and his hope for the relationship through gifts and gestures like the dinner. And thankfully, she was gracious and didn't pursue it. For the rest of the evening, they laughed and talked about grad-school possibilities and other dreams they'd tucked away. Trevor went away feeling so grateful that Abbie was in his life and happy that the night had been a total success.

However, when they met up for lunch a few days later, Abbie was obviously tense and distant. Even though he grabbed her and swung her around the way he'd done before their big anniversary date, this time she was unreceptive and not giggling. When he asked what was wrong, she said, "Nothing. I'm fine. I just think we need to talk. There's a guy at work asking me to a concert, and I think I might go." Trevor was stunned at this bombshell coming out of nowhere. What was going on?

Case Study Questions

1. Men: What do you think is going through Abbie's mind? Why could she suddenly be distant and consider going to a concert with another guy?

2. Women: What do you think is going through Abbie's mind? Why do you think she is distant and considering going to a concert with another guy?

3. At their lunch date, Trevor pulled the same lever he had pulled at their anniversary date (he grabbed her and swung her around), but he got a difference response. Is that randomness, or is there a reason?

4. Men: How can Abbie share what is going on in a way that Trevor will receive it well, instead of making things worse?

Bringing It Home
Discussing It Privately with Her

- Have I ever made it hard for you to share what you were really thinking?
- What can I do to make it easier for you to share what you are truly thinking and feeling and what you need?

My Notes

My **Notes**

Part 1: Understanding Men

Respect

Why Your Respect Means More to Him than Even Your Affection

Your respect means more to your man than even your affection. Three out of four men would rather feel alone and unloved than inadequate and disrespected. Men need to be respected—in public and in private—in the areas of their judgment, abilities, communication, and assumptions. It's not about male pride; it's about assuaging feelings of inadequacy. And your man's highest need is feeling that you trust him, regardless. You can help by assuming the best and choosing to demonstrate respect for him even when he makes mistakes, just as you want him to love you unconditionally.

For this discussion, both men and women should read chapter 2 in the *For Women Only* book and/or watch session 2, part 1 of the *For Couples Only* video study.

Key Questions

1. Do you agree with the premise that giving a man unconditional respect (even if he messes up sometimes) is just as important as giving a woman unconditional love (even if she is unlovable sometimes)? Why?

2. Can you think of any examples (either in real life or in movies or television) of women who regularly and sincerely say "I love you" yet inadvertently show their men subtle (or not-so-subtle) signals of disrespect?

3. Have you seen women who do a good job of showing their men trust and respect? What are some of the things they do that stand out to you?

Case Study

Ron and Elizabeth were in the car, heading to meet friends for a movie in an unfamiliar area of town. Everything was going fine until they got closer and found themselves in a maze of unfamiliar streets—and they didn't have a GPS.

Elizabeth asked Ron to stop and ask for directions. He grinned and said, "I can find it!" And he continued to navigate the maze, peering at street signs in the gathering darkness.

Three or four minutes later, Elizabeth became worried and impatient. "Now, really," she said, "don't be stubborn. Let's just stop at that gas station over there, and I'll run in and ask." Ron's grin faded. Without a word, he pulled over so she could hop out. A few moments later, she was back in the car, directing him to the right street. Ron didn't say much as they walked to the theater to greet their friends. Elizabeth could tell that something was wrong, but she wasn't sure what.

Case Study Questions

1. Women: Put yourself in Ron's shoes. What was he thinking when Elizabeth asked him to stop and ask the first time? the second time?

2. Men: What would you like to share about what you would be thinking the first time? the second time?

3. What could Elizabeth and Ron each have done differently to allow for a happier outcome? Would that have been the right thing to do? the wrong thing to do?

Bringing It Home
Discussing It Privately with Him

- What in my actions or words most makes you feel respected and appreciated? disrespected and inadequate? If I could change just one thing about how I relate to you in this area, what would you most want it to be?
- Can you give me an example of a time I really made you feel trusted or appreciated? a time when you felt that I didn't trust or respect you?
- Confidentially, which of the couples we know have respectful behavior patterns and which do not?

--- My **Notes** ---

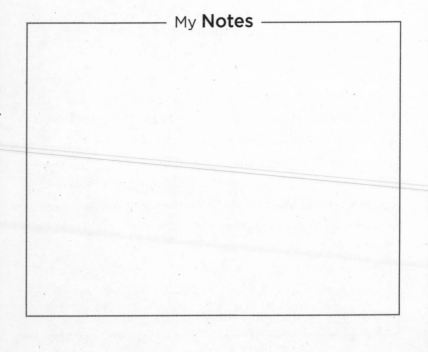

Part 2: Understanding Women

Reassurance

Why Her "I Do"
Will Always Mean
"Do You?"

Even if your relationship is great, your spouse (or girlfriend) likely has a fundamental insecurity about your love. Her feelings of insecurity are surprisingly frequent, intensely painful, and—to the male mind—paradoxically resistant to logic. When her insecurity is triggered by conflict between you or your withdrawal, she may respond in ways that confuse or dismay you. But when you're clued in, those puzzling behaviors serve as red warning lights signaling you to respond to her need by verbally reassuring her of your love and by actively pursuing her to show that you would choose her all over again.

For this discussion, both men and women should read chapter 2 in the *For Men Only* book and/or watch session 2, part 2 of the *For Couples Only* video study.

Key Questions

1. Knowing there isn't a "permanently loved" switch in a woman's heart, what are some things a man can do to give a woman regular assurance that she is loved?

2. Women: Can you explain what it does for you to hear assurance that you are loved, even if your man feels awkward saying it? Give some examples of what you've heard or experienced that made you feel very loved.

3. Women: Since reassurance is often most needed right when a man feels least like giving it (for example, times of conflict), what can he do to give you that reassurance in a way that he can manage at that point? (Men: Chime in on what works!)

Case Study

Shelly and Brian loved each other deeply, but they were in a diffi-cult season. Their family business was struggling and both had been working long hours, as well as juggling care for two young children under the age of four. They were snapping at each other a lot due to stress.

They were also approaching the annual summer period where

Shelly took the kids and spent a month at her parents' beach house. Brian usually made the five-hour drive to see them a couple of weekends during the month, but other than that he stayed home to keep the business running.

The night before Shelly left for the annual trip, they had their biggest argument yet and both had hurt feelings, which they were unable to resolve before she loaded the kids in the car the next morning. Brian also let her know he probably couldn't come to the beach house that year, since he had to keep his nose to the grindstone. They gave each other a rather stilted hug and a kiss, but as Shelly drove away, tears trickled down her face.

Case Study Questions

1. Men: Put yourself in Shelly's shoes. What might be going through her mind as she drives away?

2. Women: What can you share about what might be going through her mind as she drives away?

3. What could Brian do to change how Shelly is feeling—either now or later?

Bringing It Home

Discussing It Privately with Her

- What are some things I might say or do that make you worry about us or about whether I truly love you? Conversely, what makes you *feel* loved?
- What does it feel like for you when we have a conflict and I shut down? When we're arguing or frustrated with each other, how can I reassure you of my love while still giving myself time to process what's happening?
- If I could change just one thing about how I relate to you in this area, what would you most want it to be?

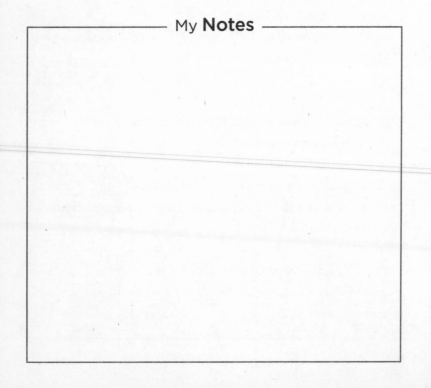

My **Notes**

Processing
When Checking Out
Is Actually Checking In

Providing
How His Need to Provide
Weighs Your Man Down, and
Why He Likes It That Way

Processing In a conflict, women tend to want to talk things out immediately, whereas men tend to retreat. Women often get hurt and view the retreat as a lack of love, but men often retreat in order to think things through and communicate well later. Guys' brains are wired to need actual time to process their thoughts and emotions well. Only then can they come back and comfortably engage in the discussion.

Providing Even if you alone earned enough income to provide for your family, it would make no difference to the mental burden your husband feels to provide. Being a provider is at the core of a man's identity. Men feel powerful when they provide, and providing is a way to express their love. Wives often get exasperated when husbands work late, which frustrates men because they think their long work hours (and the income that comes with them) are saying "I love you." Women can help by choosing not to nag, by contributing to the family budget (if that is consistent with the family's shared career decisions), and by refusing to engage in unnecessary spending. Or, if they earn more, by ensuring their husbands feel appreciated as a provider, regardless.

For this discussion, since part 1 of this session covers two subjects, both men and women should read chapters 4 and 5 in the *For Women Only* book and/or watch session 3, part 1 of the *For Couples Only* video study.

Key Questions

Processing

1. Men: If you are one who does go underground to process thoughts and feelings, is it that you don't *want* to talk about something or that you *can't* talk about something? or both?

2. How can a woman ask a necessary question without making the man feel that she is (a) challenging him or (b) pushing him before he is ready?

Providing

1. If you are comfortable doing so, give an example of a time when a woman may have added to a man's sense of provider burden or not appreciated the depth of it. Give an example of when the woman got it right.

2. Men: How often is the idea of providing for your family (or being the provider) in the back of your mind? Does it change, depending on your financial situation?

Case Study

This case study is a continuation of the one in session 1, part 1. Please reread that case (on page 99) before continuing on here.

As they left the restaurant, Barb could see that Grant was clearly wrestling with feeling angry and wanting to withdraw from her. She asked what was wrong, and he said, "You know how much I have wanted a way to get back into music. And I feel like you just stomped on my dream. And you humiliated me in front of our friends."

Now it was her turn to be frustrated. "Well, why did you drop something so big like that without telling me? Why didn't you talk it through with me before?"

Case Study Questions

1. Men: Was what Grant said actually dropping something big on Barb? Was it a comment that was meant to be taken seriously as a likely change of life direction?

2. Will Grant be more or less likely to dream in front of Barb next time?

3. Rewind: If we could change how this unfolded, how could Barb have responded in a way that would feel safe and respectful to Grant, even while she was surprised?

Bringing It Home
Discussing It Privately with Him

Processing

- Do I ever make you feel cornered in conversation when you really need to process instead? What, specifically, would help?
- If I am troubled by needing a response within a reasonable period of time (whatever that looks like), how can I honor your need to process but still talk it through or get the answer in the way *I* need?

Providing

- Have I ever made you feel that financial security was more important to me than having you and the closeness of our relationship? Can you help me understand some of the things I do that make you feel that way?
- Do you feel like you're doing a difficult balancing act, providing and making time to be available to the family?

What can I do to help make things better or easier for you in these areas?

- [If the wife is the primary income earner] Does it bother you that I earn more? Help me understand what it feels like for you. How can I show you how much I appreciate what you do to provide (including the provision of being a great dad and so on)?

My **Notes**

Part 2: Understanding Women

Security
How Your Provider/Protector Instinct Can Leave Her Feeling More Unsafe and Less Cared For

Listening
Why Her Feeling About the Problem Is the Problem, and How to Fix Your Urge to Fix

Security While most men think that a woman wants financial security, what she wants even more is emotional security. That is, she wants to feel close to you, to know that she's your non-work-time priority, to know you're committed to her, and to have you involved at home. And although she does want financial security, wants you to be fulfilled in your work, and appreciates your efforts to provide, she'd willingly endure financial struggles if that's what it took to have more of you (for example, if you wanted a lower-paying, more family-friendly job). Fortunately, building emotional security and closeness is easier than you might think. Making small gestures of love and spending discretionary hours with her and at home will go a long way.

Listening When a woman voices an emotional concern, a man's first instinct is to set aside her emotions, identify the technical problem, and fix it. But what she needs first is for you to give her your full attention, set aside the technical problem, and instead listen to and validate what she's feeling about it. By restating her concern and telling her it's okay to feel that way, you will actually fix a problem for her—the emotional one that needs to be addressed before she will be interested in actually tackling the technical one. As you learn to listen in the way she needs, you may sometimes feel that she's blaming you, when in fact she probably appreciates you more than you realize.

For this discussion, since this discussion covers two subjects, intertwined, both men and women should read chapters 5 and 6 in the *For Men Only* book and/or watch session 3, part 2 of the *For Couples Only* video study.

Key Questions

Security

1. Men: Do you ever feel like you're caught between a rock (her need for your time and closeness) and a hard place (her need for financial security)?

2. Women: Are both equally important to you? If one had to give, which one would it be?

Listening

1. Why do you think it's difficult for men to forget the fix and instead focus on a woman's feelings, especially during a conflict? In what situation is a fix important?

2. Women: How do you feel when he sets the fix aside for the moment and does listen to your feelings? If one occurs to you, share an example of your man doing just that, and describe what happened in your heart as a result.

Case Study

The Lewis and Connor families had been best friends for years and were sharing a week at a luxurious beach house owned by the Lewis family. Lucas Lewis was reading his novel on the screened-in porch when he overheard his wife, Liz, and Cheryl Connor talking by the pool below. Cheryl asked wistfully, "Ah, Liz... How does it feel to have all your financial needs met? to never worry about money? to have this beautiful vacation house anytime you want to come? I just can't imagine..."

Lucas was proud when his wife chuckled and said, "I know, I love this house!" But then, shocked, he heard his wife's voice grow wistful in turn. "But honestly, Cheryl...I think you're the rich one. Truly. I see how Carl treats you. He gets you. He rubs your feet when you're watching TV. He tells you how beautiful you are. He sympathizes when you tell him story after story about frustrating things that happened with your boss that day. Do you know how many women would kill to get a guy like that?"

Lucas tossed his novel aside and took off for a long beach run. He couldn't help feeling angry about his wife's words. After all, hadn't he busted his tail and worked crazy hours to run a successful business so he could give Liz everything she could possibly want? Was she now dissing a decade of his self-sacrifice and saying she would have preferred long foot rubs and nights on the couch sharing meaningless stories? Would he ever be able to please his wife?

Case Study Questions

1. Men: What would you be thinking if you were Lucas? Can you relate to his frustration? Now put yourself in Liz's shoes. What, specifically, is she wistful about?

2. Women: What do you think Liz is wistful about?

3. Is it possible that Liz is wistful about the nonfinancial things because she already has the financial security? Is she simply not appreciating all that she already has? Are providing stuff and providing emotional security necessarily mutually exclusive? Could it have been possible for Lucas to provide both for Liz?

Bringing It Home

Discussing It Privately with Her

Security

- If you had to choose, which is more important to you: financial security or emotional security? As the most extreme example, would you rather endure financial hardship or a lack of closeness between us?

Listening

- What kind of listener am I? Do I "jump to the fix," or do I seem to care about how you feel first?
- How can I be a better listener to you in general? What words or body language can I use that would convey to you how much I care?

My Notes

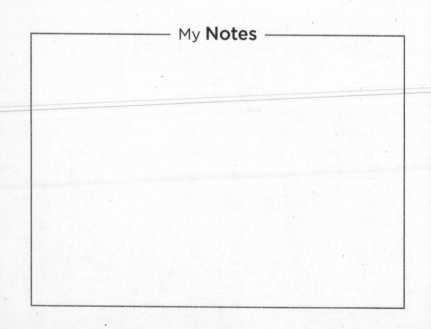

My **Notes**

Part 1: Understanding Men

Sex

Why Sex Unlocks a Man's Emotions (Guess Who Holds the Key?)

Your sexual desire for your husband profoundly affects his sense of well-being and confidence in all areas of his life. Men want to be wanted, and three out of four would still feel empty if their wives weren't both sexually engaged and sexually satisfied. If this area is lacking, a man feels a deep sense of personal rejection and even depression. It usually takes an overt decision for a woman to get tuned in, involved, passionate, creative, and committed to ensuring that her husband feels desired by her.

For this discussion, both men and women should read chapter 6 in the *For Women Only* book and/or watch session 4, part 1 of the *For Couples Only* video study.

Key Questions

1. Women: Were you surprised that men say that sex is so much more than a physical need?

2. In real life, or even in movies or television, what examples have you seen of how a man who feels desired is more confident in other areas of his life? and how a man who isn't feeling desired feels a lack of well-being?

3. Both men and women want to feel close, and neither likes to have distance. Women often want to be emotionally close first, in order to consider making love. Are men the reverse, at times? Do they want to pursue sex *in order to* feel close?

4. Men: What would you most want to explain to women about the impact of a man feeling desired by his wife?

Case Study

On Friday night, Josh finished up a series of high-powered, stressful meetings at the office, jumped into his car, and made his way through the congested rush-hour traffic. He stopped at the florist and smiled as he picked up a small bouquet of flowers for his wife, Kayla. Due to an insane schedule of kids' activities, they hadn't had much intimate time together recently, and she'd said a few days earlier that she was sure hoping the weekend was a better time for it. As he thought of her, he was feeling a strong desire for her and for that closeness and reconnection.

When he got home, however, Kayla was showing no signs that

the stress had abated. The kids had been fighting, her boss was a jerk, the sink was dripping, the cat had thrown up on the new rug, and the roast was burned. When the couple finally crawled into bed that night, Josh reached over to touch his wife, but she yawned, turned away, and muttered, "G'night, honey. Love you." It seemed to Josh that sleep was once again the winning priority for his wife. Had she not noticed his attempts at romance and his not-so-subtle suggestions about wanting sex?

Case Study Questions

1. Women: Put yourself in Josh's shoes. How would you be feeling? What might you conclude about your desirability?

2. Men: How would you be feeling if you were Josh?

3. What could Kayla have done differently? What could Josh have done differently? What difference would it make if Kayla understood how Josh felt?

4. Men: Women often say exhaustion is a roadblock to wanting to be intimate—which many men find hard to imagine. Can you imagine it if you compared it to something that would be a roadblock for you? For example, would it be a roadblock for you if your wife had been repeatedly critical of you that day?

Bringing It Home
Discussing It Privately with Him

- How do I make you feel about yourself in the area of intimacy? What are some things I do (or can do) to let you know how much I do desire you?
- When I say "not tonight" because I am simply too tired or preoccupied, do you feel that I am rejecting you? If so, how can I communicate my inability to you without sending that rejection message? What would help?
- What is your ideal frequency of sex?

My **Notes**

Part 2: Understanding Women

Sex

How Her Desires Are Impacted by Her Unique Wiring, and Why Your Ego Shouldn't Be

Most women tend to crave sex less often than men do, and it's usually not because the woman doesn't desire her husband. A woman's sexual wiring is distinctly different from a man's, with a different hormone mix, a more emotional (instead of visual) orientation, and a physical and mental need for anticipation time. Often she's as frustrated as you are by the sexual differences between you and would change those factors if she could. The good news is, often just a few simple changes can propel you toward the kind of sexual relationship both of you want. These include building the day-to-day closeness she needs outside the bedroom, flirting with her (again, outside the bedroom) so she knows she's attractive and desirable and you'd choose her all over again, and letting her know what's on your menu for the evening well before you step into the bedroom.

For this discussion, both men and women should read chapter 7 in the *For Men Only* book and/or watch session 4, part 2 of the *For Couples Only* video study.

Key Questions

1. Women: Men have often heard that "sex begins in the kitchen" and they need to do thoughtful things. But just because he is doing sweet, kind, thoughtful things, will his wife necessarily be thinking about physical intimacy later? Do you think most women need anticipation time?

2. What difference would it make to have anticipation time, for either men or women? Does a woman needing anticipation time mean she doesn't desire her man? Why not?

3. When a woman desires her man but truly is too tired, how can she say "Not tonight, honey" without hurting his feelings? Is it possible?

Case Study

Kim's birthday was last week, and after a long week of overtime, she finally carved out a few hours to treat herself to clothes shopping, which she hadn't been able to do for almost a year. She bought one outfit with a birthday gift card and splurged on another one.

When she came home from the mall around seven o'clock, her teenage daughter giggled and looked through her bags. "Oh, Mom, you finally got some cool clothes for your birthday! Hey, try this on!" Kim did so and returned quickly, sashaying into the living room to show off her outfit for her daughter and her husband, Kevin. Her daughter clapped and whistled at the outfit, but Kevin seemed distracted by the price tags. He didn't seem to be in a great mood and asked what was for dinner. Hastily, Kim changed into jeans.

"Okay, I'll get dinner on," she said with a sigh.

A few hours later Kevin came up to bed wearing his favorite boxers, which meant that he was ready for some fun. He said, "Sorry I was a bit grumpy earlier. The big deal at work was going south, but I just got an e-mail from my boss that it is back on. Whew." He gave her a grin. "You looked smokin' hot in that outfit. Now get over here—" But Kim simply turned the light out and pulled the covers up to her chin. The temperature in the room had just dropped a full ten degrees.

Case Study Questions

1. Men: What happened here? Put yourself in Kim's shoes. Talk about some reasons she wasn't too hot to trot in bed that night.

2. Women: Do you spot multiple issues that set this night up to be a chilly one? List them.

3. Should Kim have been able to just shake it off and respond after his apology?

4. Women: Even if Kevin had responded perfectly to the outfit, would that have been enough? Assume that Kevin wasn't grumpy and said, "That outfit looks nice on you." If you're Kim, are you thinking about sex? Now assume that after Kevin says, "That outfit looks nice on you," the daughter leaves the room, and he steps close to grin and whisper, "I'd love to see what's under it later." Would that change how the evening ends?

Bringing It Home
Discussing It Privately with Her

- Does it make a difference in your emotional or physical interest level if you have some time to anticipate intimacy? What suggestions do you have for how I could give you that anticipation time?
- Pretend you have a magic wand. If you could wave it to make a day of sweet intimacy that ends with sex, what would that day look like—from start to end?
- Do you need that sense of closeness outside the bedroom in order to want to be close inside the bedroom? What are some things I do to make you feel that closeness? What else can I do to help us build that closeness?

My **Notes**

Part 1: Understanding Men

Visual

Why It's So Natural for Him to Look and So Hard to Forget What He's Seen

Even happily married, devoted men are instinctively tempted to look at eye-magnet women, and most men's brains have something like a mental picture file of stored female images that can intrude upon their thoughts without warning. As upsetting as these truths might be to some women, remember that temptation is not sin, and your guy is likely trying his best to minimize those involuntary thoughts and win the battle of the mind. The lure doesn't happen because of you and has nothing to do with his feelings for you; in fact, most men wish they didn't have it! As women, we can be supportive of our men's efforts to keep their thought lives pure, pray for them, and champion modesty. We can also realize that (as awkward as it can be to hear), he feels cared for when we make an effort to take care of ourselves for him. Conversely, when we don't make that effort, he feels we don't care about him. In all this, we can realize God created men to be visual and that His creation is good.

For this discussion, both men and women should read chapter 7 (and perhaps chapter 9, which is briefly referenced in the video) in the *For Women Only* book and/or watch session 5, part 1 of the *For Couples Only* video study.

Key Questions

1. Women: Does learning about the brain wiring of men change how you think about a man's visual nature and the impact of being visual? How so?

2. Men: What is it like to live in this culture and be bombarded with images that you were never supposed to see?

3. At what point does a biological, automatic temptation become sin? Where does a line get crossed? What do you think were some of God's intentions in creating men as visually oriented creatures?

4. Do you think it is really true that men love women's individuality and don't expect them to look like the supermodels on television?

Case Study

Jackson and Larry were sitting across the table from each other at Starbucks, discussing work. Jackson noticed that Larry had a tendency to look at every woman who walked in—usually starting at the feet but moving swiftly up all the available real estate. Jackson also noticed the women coming in and out but tried to keep his eyes focused on Larry.

Finally, a very attractive woman passed by, wearing tight, low-cut clothing that displayed all her assets. She sat at a table just off Jackson's left shoulder where Larry could see her easily and Jackson could see her if he turned his head fully to the side—which he didn't do. For the next thirty minutes, Larry rarely made eye contact with his colleague. For some reason his gaze was fixed just over Jackson's left shoulder.

Case Study Questions

1. Women: What do you think is going through Jackson's mind as he drinks his coffee and talks about business, while Miss Starbucks is sitting behind his left shoulder?

2. Men: What would you say is going through Jackson's mind in that situation?

3. What do you think all the women walking into the coffee shop feel about Larry's attention? What do you think Miss Starbucks thinks of it?

4. Men: Suppose Larry was a close personal friend, not a colleague. Do you feel sorry that he has so fully given in to temptation—and is feeding it? If you discover that he has never been coached on how to handle visual temptation, what advice might you give to help him with this struggle?

Bringing It Home
Discussing It Privately with Him

Note: Because this can be a difficult subject for husbands and wives to discuss, please approach it with discretion and compassion—including skipping the section if your spouse/significant other prefers not to talk about it. For some couples, it will be better to discuss it with the help of a trained counselor.

- Can you help me understand what it is like when a very attractive, skimpily dressed woman appears in a man's line of sight? Do you feel visually bombarded in this culture?
- Do you feel free to share your struggles or needs with me in this area? How can I best support you in this area?

— My **Notes** —

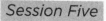

Part 2: Understanding Women

Beauty

What the Little Girl Inside Your Woman Is Dying to Hear from You—and How to Guard Your Answer Well

A woman is unlikely to outgrow the little-girl need to hear that you—the man in her life—find her beautiful. She's bombarded daily with demeaning images and messages, and she has a deeply rooted need to be assured of your passionate attraction to her. You can counteract negative internal dialogue and external pressure by frequently and sincerely telling her she's beautiful to you, budgeting for her efforts to feel beautiful, and deliberately avoiding the impulse to let your eyes or thoughts dwell on other women.

For this discussion, both men and women should read chapter 8 in the *For Men Only* book and/or watch session 5, part 2 of the *For Couples Only* video study.

Key Questions

1. What is the one big question a woman is asking her man when she shows off an outfit or asks how she looks? How can a guy answer the unspoken question in her heart?

2. Women: How important is it really for a woman to be told she's beautiful? What does it do for a woman to hear this from her man? Is there anything a man can do to better meet this need? anything that makes it worse?

3. Is there ever a time when a woman needs to be able to ask a technical question ("Does this look okay on me?") and get a technical answer ("Honestly, it doesn't flatter you. The other outfit was better.")? How can a guy answer that question safely?

Case Study

More than two years after the birth of their second child, Nicole still hadn't lost all her pregnancy weight. Blake noticed that she tended to dress quickly when he was present and seemed embarrassed about her body. She occasionally muttered comments about gravity taking a toll or about pregnancy having left its mark. When she said things like "Now you're married to a fat old lady" or "I wish

I could be beautiful for you again," he cringed and protested stumblingly. In truth, he did wish she'd lose the excess weight, but he didn't know how to encourage her without causing further pain. And regardless, nothing could change the fact that he still became excited by her body, got lost in her deep brown eyes (especially when she smiled that smile), and constantly thought about making love with her—even if it was hard to find the time these days.

Case Study Questions

1. Men: Put yourself in Nicole's shoes. If it is true that inside Nicole is a little girl who still wants to be affirmed as pretty by the most important man in her life, how does she feel about herself in a culture saturated with countless media images of how women "should" look?

2. What does she need from her man? What do you think Nicole is longing to hear when she makes a disparaging comment about herself? Is there any downside to Blake's saying what Nicole is longing to hear? Why or why not?

3. What would it feel like to Nicole if she noticed Blake's eyes lingering on another woman's figure? What message would play in her head? Alternatively, how would she feel if Blake turned away from other attractive women, communicating that "I only have eyes for you"? Would she even notice?

Bringing It Home
Discussing It Privately with Her

- I want to make sure you know I find you beautiful. What do I say or do that makes you feel that way?
- Will you be honest and tell me how my words and actions make you feel about yourself? Does anything I do or say hurt you? Are there some things I could start doing—or stop doing—that would let you know even more how much you rock my world?

—— My **Notes** ——

Part 1: Understanding Men

Romance

Why the Reluctant Romeo You Know Really Does Want Romance

Your man really does want romance, but he may feel as though he has poor skills in this area. Or he may simply have different ideas about what is romantic. Most men would like more romance—yes, even apart from sex! Men want connection, fun, and togetherness as much as women do. A guy often views taking romantic initiative as a huge risk for humiliation or inadequacy, so you need to encourage him and prove that he's not at risk. Most men also view going out and doing things together as romantic.

For this discussion, both men and women should read chapter 8 in the *For Women Only* book and/or watch session 6, part 1 of the *For Couples Only* video study.

Key Questions

1. What are some reasons men might not act on the romantic thoughts and ideas they say they have? Have you ever seen exam-

ples of men trying to be romantic and then, feeling the attempt wasn't good enough, deciding to be safe and not trying again?

2. Men: What do men want most—what are they looking for—when they ask their wives or girlfriends to accompany them on little outings, errands, or adventures?

3. Knowing how guys are wired, what are some creative, sensitive things a woman can do to affirm her man's attempts at romance?

Case Study

Destiny and James were bustling around, getting ready for a movie date and trying to get out the door on time. Destiny was struggling with her hair and glancing at the clock every two minutes. "It took me a lot of time to plan this evening," she said in irritation, "and I wish I was not the one who always had to do it."

James looked at his wife for a long moment. Then he forced himself to smile ruefully. "Don't look at me. I've learned my lesson."

Startled, Destiny asked what he meant, but James just shrugged and mumbled something about the beach weekend last year and the last few times he tried to arrange a dinner date. When she pressed him to explain, he shook his head. "Listen, it's just better that you do it. That way you get it the way you want it."

Case Study Questions

1. Women: Put yourself in James's shoes. Why isn't he planning dates?

2. Men: Explain how James feels. Why is "not getting it the way she wants it" such a big deal for a guy?

3. What should a woman do when something isn't the way she wants it and yet she doesn't want to shut her man down?

4. Now that the situation has unfolded as it has, what can Destiny do, if anything, to change things and encourage James to try again?

Bringing It Home

Discussing It Privately with Him

- How am I doing in the area of affirming you for any attempts you have made to do something romantic?
- Have I ever done something to make you think I didn't appreciate your romantic efforts? If so, can you forgive me? How can we start over?
- What are your favorite things to do for a "togetherness" outing?

My **Notes**

Part 2: Understanding Women

Emotions (Windows)

What You Should Know About the Fabulous Female Brain

Men generally focus on one thing at a time, compartmentalizing other thoughts and feelings for later consideration. But most women experience multiple thoughts and emotions at the same time, and these thoughts and emotions can't easily be dismissed. Many women are blindsided regularly by current worries or by negative, unresolved thoughts and feelings from the recent or far past. Sudden shifts in topic, introduction of "ancient history," or flashes of emotion often signal a past or current concern that keeps invading a woman's awareness even if she doesn't want it there. These concerns are like pop-up windows on a computer, and you can help close those windows by encouraging her to talk out and/or resolve whatever concern is popping up—or even by taking some action to resolve it for her.

For this discussion, both men and women should read chapter 3 in the *For Men Only* book and/or watch session 6, part 2 of the *For Couples Only* video study.

Key Questions

1. Women: Give an example of a type of thought that you would have difficulty closing out and that you would have to take some action to resolve.

2. Women: Would it help you if your husband or boyfriend said, "Do you have an open window that is bugging you? What would make you feel better? Is there anything I can do to help you close that window?"

3. Men understandably get frustrated when they think an issue is done with and it comes back "out of nowhere" days later. Why does that happen, and is there any way it can be prevented?

Case Study

Maria and one of her close friends had a major argument right before the friend left on vacation. That evening, Maria told Isaac the story and described several things her friend said that really hurt her feelings.

The next day, after Maria brought it up again several times, Isaac said, "Honey, you're good friends. I'm sure you two will work it out when she gets back. But since you can't do anything about it now, just put it out of your mind."

Case Study Questions

1. Men: Explain why Isaac thought that was the best advice to give Maria. If you were Isaac, what would be going through your mind when you urge Maria to put something out of her mind?

2. Do you think that Maria is just obsessing about something inappropriately?

3. Women: What do you think went through Maria's mind when Isaac told Maria to "just put it out of your mind"? What could Isaac have said instead?

Bringing It Home

Discussing It Privately with Her

- If something is bugging you, what can I do to help you close the window?
- When you're bothered by something, do you want me to say "If it will make you feel better, go ahead and address it"?

- Are there some open windows you normally handle that
  you would be willing to trust me with? (And are you okay
  if I don't do it exactly the way that you would do it?)

Going Forward with Your Mate

Before you conclude your final time together, please allow a few minutes
to ask each other the question below. Note your answer in the space pro-
vided and make a commitment to your mate to try to meet this one need.

> Out of all the subjects we've talked about together
> over these last few weeks, what is *one* thing
> I can do that will make you feel most cared for?

As we wrap up our journey together, we are grateful for your investment of time over these last weeks—which truly is an investment in each
other and in your relationship. As you move forward, our prayer is that
you will see great return on this investment and experience the fullness of
joy that God intends for our marriages and relationships.

Enjoy the continuing journey!

My **Notes**

Want her to REALLY understand you?

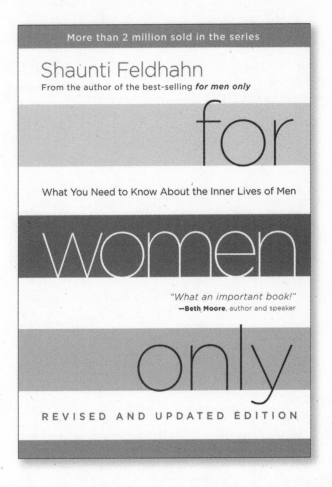

For Women Only offers fascinating insights into the hidden lives of men. Based upon a landmark nationwide poll, Shaunti Feldhahn offers groundbreaking information and advises how to convert her findings into practical application.

Read an excerpt from this book and more at
www.WaterBrookMultnomah.com

Finally.
You Can Understand Her

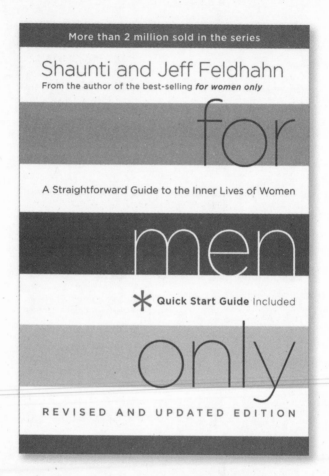

What makes her tick? What is she really asking (but not actually saying)? Take the guesswork out of trying to please your wife or girlfriend and begin loving her in the way she needs. Easily. *For Men Only* is a straightforward map that will lead you straight into her heart.

Shaunti Feldhahn Showed You How Men Think At Home —Now Find Out What They Think At Work

Do you know the unwritten rules of the workplace? *For Women Only in the Workplace* will equip you to be an effective Christian business-woman no matter what your circumstances.

Also available from Shaunti!